In the Temple of Wolves

A Winter's Immersion
in Wild Yellowstone

Rick Lamplugh

Some chapters of this book first appeared in different versions in
the following literary journals:
Composite Arts Magazine: "Vanity at Trout Lake"
Gold Man Review: "How Death Feeds Life"
Shoal: "The Bison's Last Ride"

Catalog information:
In the Temple of Wolves: A Winter's Immersion in Wild Yellowstone / Rick Lamplugh.—1st edition.
1. Yellowstone National Park—Description and travel. 2. Ecology—Yellowstone National Park.
3. Natural History—Yellowstone National Park. 4. Lamplugh,
Rick.—Journeys. 5. Lamplugh, Rick, 1948-

ISBN: 1490372059
ISNB 13: 9781490372051

Printed in the United States of America on library quality stock
10 9 8 7 6 5 4 3 2 1

What Others Say about
In the Temple of Wolves

———

I admire the honesty of Rick Lamplugh's experiences: personal foibles of stumbling with his snowshoes or getting lost at Trout Lake, the full range of emotions welling up while watching a bison calf slowly die or an elk being hunted relentlessly. As soon as I finished *In the Temple of Wolves*, I wanted to share it immediately! *Terry Donnelly*

In *In the Temple of Wolves*, Rick weaves together the beauty, the life and death struggles, the mundane, and the extraordinary to capture the magic that is the Lamar Valley experience. *Anita Edington*

I was so impressed with the amount of research done for this book. It mixes in the science along with personal observations and experiences to tell a story. Rick Lamplugh captures the magic and draw of this special place, the wildness, the sense of adventure, the wonder of nature. *Karen Withrow*

The book made me wistful for the time I have spent at the Lamar Buffalo Ranch, and allowed me to happily relive some memories of the time I have spent in the valley. It also made me want to quit my job!!!! *Tracy Arthur*

More than anyplace else, Yellowstone is about moments; moments of revelation for each and every student of the natural world. Through his story telling, Rick brings to light some of these remarkable moments from this most remarkable place! *Leo Leckie*

I got up at sunrise and sat on our screened porch to read a couple more chapters of this wonderful book. I have enjoyed each and every story Rick Lamplugh told. He has a wonderful way of putting his thoughts and feelings down on paper. *Len Carolan*

Through Rick, we experience life and death, joy and fear. We get to watch as people experience the sights and sounds of the Lamar for the first time, of seeing and hearing a wolf for the first time. *Sue Timm*

This book took me into the valley as if I were there. I saw what Rick Lamplugh saw and could relate to the cold temperatures and deep snows he so eloquently described. I heard the wolves howl as he did and could picture them across the valley. I was with him when he pulled the bison carcass into the valley and examined what was left a few weeks later. *Chuck Snover*

For Mary

The Lamar Buffalo Ranch

Table of Contents

———

1

Hunger and Delight

In the middle of the night, I slip from the warm log cabin into the below-zero temperature outside. I pull the door closed, hoping not to wake my wife, Mary. Still, the click of the latch resounds in the silence of the wild. I crunch onto the ice- and snow-covered path, excited to be alone with the night. Frigid air freezes my nose hairs and burns my lungs. A full yellow-orange moon, dark craters obvious, turns scattered clouds tangerine.

Though I wear a headlamp, I leave the light off; I don't want my vision trapped in a narrow, bouncing cone. Instead, my eyes adjust to reflected moonlight as I meander toward the bunkhouse, scanning for bison. A herd surrounded our cabin yesterday, swinging their massive heads side to side, bulldozing through the snow, hungry for dried grasses that provide the nutrition of an empty cereal box. Mary and I, kneeling on our bed, watched and whispered and pointed, our smiling faces pressed against cold window panes.

To my right, a branch of Rose Creek bubbles by on its way to the Lamar River. The creek forms two of the three borders of the historic Lamar Buffalo Ranch in this remote northeastern corner of Yellowstone National Park. We arrived three days ago and will live and work here all winter as volunteer Program Assistants, helping the Yellowstone Association Institute deliver field seminars. Visitors will come from many countries to participate in these multi-day classes taught by experts on flora, fauna, geology, history, and photography.

For a stipend of twelve dollars per day—even on our days off—we each drive a fourteen-passenger bus wherever the seminar instructor directs us. At the end of the ranch's driveway, we can turn east or west on the narrow road that runs fifty-two miles from park headquarters in Mammoth, past the ranch, and out of the park to Silver Gate, a community with a year-round population of eleven to sixteen, depending on who you ask. This is the only road in this section of the park that is plowed and kept open all year. The Lamar Buffalo Ranch and a ranger station eleven miles away are the sole winter residences along that road.

When an instructor directs us into a roadside pullout, the next part of our job begins. We park the bus, help set up spotting scopes, and make sure participants spot wildlife. We ensure that everyone is safe by discouraging risky behavior such as a participant setting up his tripod in the middle of the road because he is so eager to photograph a wolf. We also accompany groups snowshoeing or cross country skiing for a wilder experience. If an emergency occurs, we provide first aid and radio for help.

When not supporting a class, we pull camp duty and shovel snow from yards and yards of paths, and clean the bunkhouse, bathhouse, and thirteen visitor cabins. Our informal motto is "clean till your fingers bleed" and that's easy to do. The work days are long and full, but listening to a world-class naturalist teach as I drive the bus or hearing a wolf howl as I shovel snow can't be beat.

I look across the moonlit parking lot where shadows of a split rail fence dip and glide over the snow. This corral once enclosed the bison that saved Yellowstone's herd—in 1901 there were fewer than two dozen bison left in the entire park. Now, after one of the most successful restorations in the world, around 4,000 bison roam the park, and the historic corral confines only the array of solar panels that help power this off-the-grid ranch.

I pass the dark bunkhouse that is guarded by two old cottonwoods and bears a name from its past: The ranch hands who tended the growing buffalo herd lived in this bunkhouse. Though no one stays there now, the building is still the heart of the ranch. It houses a classroom, library, and commercial kitchen where staff and visitors fix their own meals.

Only six of us live here all winter—four volunteers, the ranch manager, and the district park ranger. When the ranch is free of seminar participants, we often congregate in the bunkhouse to enjoy communal dinners, conversation, board games, or to view photographs of someone's adventure. We live in simplicity here, with an easy feeling of togetherness, making fast friends from perfect strangers.

Over the crunch of my boots on snow, I hear howling— the sound that I longed for when I slid out of our warm bed. I stop, lean forward, and cup a hand behind one ear. My breath forms a gossamer curtain between me and the moon. Those wolves are here because of a wildly successful reintroduction involving the ranch, and their haunting calls—drifting in the moonlight—thrill me.

The Lamar Valley, just two miles wide, seven miles long, and called the Serengeti of North America, offers some of the best wildlife watching in the world. Winter-hungry elk and bison migrate here to graze through snow that is shallower than elsewhere in the park. Wolves, coyotes, and mountain lions stalk the grazers while eagles, ravens, and magpies wait to scavenge. The snowy backdrop makes this saga of death and life easy to spot.

When I reach the moonlit road, I turn east toward Silver Gate. Like the bison, I walk the middle. The road is not plowed after dark; tonight's snow is unmarred by car tracks. But I follow a trail of wolf tracks—some as large as my hand with fingers spread—hoping for a sighting, but that is unlikely. Wolves want nothing to do with humans; if wolves are nearby, they will catch my scent or hear me and vanish like spirits in the night.

I stop about a quarter mile from the ranch, where Rose Creek passes under the road, a wavy black ribbon reflecting the full moon. The warmer air rising from the creek cools to a ghostly haze that curves across the valley floor. Beside the creek, cottonwoods rise, filigreed branches lacing a black web across golden light and white mist.

I slide gloved hands into the warmth of my pockets and start turning a slow circle to take all this in. Across the valley floor, 8500-foot Specimen Ridge rises into the moon's glow with cirrus clouds just above, horsetails racing eastward and promising more snow. Along the ridgeline, silhouetted individual evergreens stand like the raised guard hairs on the neck of a young wolf. From the base of Specimen Ridge back to the road, the valley floor is cloaked by a blanket of snow dotted by tips of sagebrush. The river that cut this valley flows hidden under ice and snow, its braided course revealed only by wide-spaced stands of cottonwoods. I turn toward the other side of the valley, to Druid Peak ascending to almost 10,000 feet. Above the peak, stars outshine the moon. The long ridge leading to the summit looks winter-walk-able, calling me, just as Yellowstone has.

Over the last nine years, Mary and I have backpacked deep into Yellowstone's backcountry, usually in fall, and often in this part of the park. We have spent time hiking noisily, sitting quietly, and trying to sleep at night while every sound outside the tent drives us to full alert. Still, with each visit I learned more and left happy. Now I have the chance to spend three months listening to and talking with experts, observing with all my senses, and digging into the hundreds of books, videos, and maps that line the shelves of the bunkhouse library. And since it's winter and the bears are sleeping, I can explore at night, something I would never do in the backcountry in fall.

I shake my head with longing. My goal while living here is to learn everything about this place, though I know that's not possible. This park, even this small valley, is too complex. Still, I yearn to understand how this ecosystem works, how the parts fit together. From the flies that buzz half-awake in the daytime warmth of our cabin to the stoic bison trapped in a race between starvation and spring. From the snow that blows in from the Pacific to the sage that spices this high desert. From the wolf packs that hunt as well-oiled machines to bring down elk to the incredible variety of beetles that scour the bones after the other scavengers are gone. What is the science behind this majesty?

The setting moon kisses Specimen Ridge. A breeze rustles the cottonwoods; Rose Creek murmurs. To the west another wolf howls, a sustained bass. From the east, comes a wavering alto reply. February's breeding season is just around the corner and the one hundred wolves that live in the park are staking claims on mates and territory.

I feel such love for this place that tears well up. And that's not good in bitter cold. I wipe the corners of my eyes and release a long sigh, my breath mingling with the creek mist. I close my eyes. I've only been here three days, and I'm already afraid that three months isn't long enough. I open my eyes, turn back toward the ranch, gaze at Druid Peak, and gasp as a meteor disappears behind it. I start walking and smile at my puffy, down-clad shadow, stark against glistening snow, accompanying me down the road past my tracks intermingled with those of wolves. When I turn into the ranch's driveway, I cross thin ice to a sound like breaking glass. Back on snow, the fine, dry granules squeak and groan under my boots, a muted metronome.

I'm chilled and longing for the warmth of Mary and the cabin. But I stop when the howling starts again. Soft at first, like the call of a single owl. Then other distinct voices join, different tones and textures, a wild chorus of hunger and delight.

2

Sensing the Valley

The packed snowshoe trail I am following is crusty hard beneath last night's powdery inch. When the crust catches the tip of my snowshoe, I pitch forward and my knee crashes through the crust, like a rock through a window. I get up, brush away snow, and laugh. This is just what I need.

Our first three weeks at the ranch have been filled with driving buses, shoveling snow, helping visitors, practicing wilderness first aid and emergency procedures, and cleaning cabins and toilets. During scattered downtime, I've managed to explore the bunkhouse library, learning about the Lamar Valley's plants, animals, and geology. I've crammed my head full of facts, and now I need to get out of the written and into the real, off the ranch and into the wild, out of my head and into my senses.

Maybe I'll snowshoe to one of the pens from which the wolves were reintroduced many years ago. Or tackle that ridge that keeps calling me toward Druid Peak, mysterious amid this morning's clouds and snowfall. I don't need to decide right away; this trail winds a lengthy distance toward both pen and peak.

When I am halfway across the narrow, snow-covered footbridge over Rose Creek, I stop to listen to its noisy riffles and admire the lush green grasses that wave beneath the icy-cold water. Along the bank, Day-Glo orange lichen highlights boulders. Crossing the footbridge, I'm officially off the ranch and on my way to the wild. I exhale a sigh of relief, visible in the cold air.

I continue ambling along the trail—stopping here and there to look, feel, smell, taste, and listen—until I reach the spot where I must choose between peak and pen. The steep slope and virgin snow leading toward Druid Peak win out.

I leave the snowshoe trail and start switchbacking and postholing—sinking into snow up to my knees, despite my snowshoes. Breath comes hard and fast. Sweat flows. Glorious!

Halfway up the slope, I rest where the snow is not creamy smooth. The surface is punctured with holes from hooves and littered with big chunks of snow, ample evidence that a solitary bison grazed here, pushing snow to and fro with its large head, desperate for a few blades of dried grass. Meager fodder for North America's largest land mammal.

For bison and other grazers, winter is a race between the end of their stores of life-giving fat and the start of spring's nutrition. Those who lose the race—the so-called winter kill—become food for the wolves, cougars, coyotes, foxes, ravens, magpies, and eagles, as well as the starved bears that emerge in spring. Those who win, who savor spring's greens, do so by living each day—each moment—as efficiently as possible.

I can learn from these animals that survive a life much harsher than any I'll ever experience. And their lessons may be more practical than those gleaned from books in the bunkhouse. I contemplate the tracks the bison left as it moved upslope. Then I picture a line of wolves I recently watched climb a hill. Each stepped precisely in the tracks of the pack mate ahead. I plant a snowshoe over a bison track and ease my weight onto it. I don't sink. I plant the other snowshoe over the next track. No postholing. I climb easily upward, thankful for the lesson and the unknown bison that broke this trail.

When the bison's trail turns away from the peak, I stop and lean against a house-sized boulder. A passing glacier dropped this erratic twenty thousand years ago when ice filled this valley all the way to the top of Druid Peak, and the spot where I am standing was under a half mile of ice. I shake my head, boggled once again by the immensity of geologic concepts. While twenty thousand years sounds like a long time, I have stood just a few miles from here in awe of rocks that are 2.6 *billion* years old, the oldest exposed rocks in Yellowstone. If twenty thousand years is an eye blink to 2.6 billion, of what significance is my minuscule time on this planet?

That question is an intellectual rabbit hole. And just what I set out to avoid today. Determined to stay within the realm of my senses, I scan the area and spot a herd of elk two ridges away, grazing between snow-flocked conifers. They nibble briefly and then raise their heads to check for wolves. They should be cautious: Wolves were reintroduced in part to help control the elk population. But it took a while for the elk to catch on. In 1998, three years after wolves returned, a researcher watched a herd of grazing elk as a wolf pack approached. The elk did not react, and the wolves—transplanted from Canada because they hunted elk—knew an easy meal when they saw one. But as years passed, those elk smart enough to survive taught their calves to be wolf wary. Textbook Darwinism.

No, not the books again! Closing my eyes, I tune into a sound like the buzz of static electricity: dry snow flakes hitting my hood. Then the croak of a soaring raven. A moment later another one calls. Is there a wolf kill nearby?

Wolves have certainly been here. Just two nights ago, Mary and I heard a knock on our cabin door and the excited whisper of another volunteer, "There's wolves out here!" We bolted out of bed, hopped into our clothes, and burst outside into a night full of snow blown horizontal by wind gusts.

A couple of cabins away, we spotted an instructor, a world-class tracker who was staying here while teaching a tracking class. This aging professor was running around in pajamas and slippers, shining a flashlight here and there, oohing and ahhing at the perfect wolf tracks left in the snow by the Lamar Canyon pack that had just passed through the ranch. He invited us to join him as he identified specific members of the pack by their tracks. When we finally returned to the warmth of our cabin, shed snow-covered clothes, and slipped back into our cocoon, Mary and I were too excited to sleep.

But from where I now stand on the slope of Druid Peak, I can't see those cabins. In fact, there's no sign of any human presence, except for the thin, winding line of my snowshoe tracks. I am standing on the slope of a mountain of debris that a volcano deposited fifty million years ago. Then, the climate here was warm and moist, similar to that of today's southeastern United States. Forests of sycamore and chestnut, redwood and dogwood, magnolia and walnut flourished.

All that remains of those forests now are fossilized trees, created during another geological mind boggler. Millions of years ago a lava flow buried an entire forest. Tens of thousands of years later the forest that had grown atop the last lava flow was covered by yet another flow. Scientists estimate that there were twenty or more forests buried here, one above the other. Specimen Ridge, the miles-long ridge that forms the southern border of the Lamar Valley, is a layer cake of lava flows and takes its name from the abundance of specimens of fossilized trees exposed in its vicinity.

I force my thoughts away from volcanic history and discover that those grazing elk have noticed me. One stands guard, her head high, ears up. While she and I stare at each other, the rest of the herd graze less and look up more. Not wanting to bother them further and reduce their odds of tasting spring, I drop to my knees and settle into snow and silence. A few moments later the guard and the rest of the herd return to grazing, and I take out my camera and begin composing, playing with images found in groupings of elk, snow, sage, and conifers. Time flows while I sit still.

When a chill brings a shiver, I rise and start to put my camera away. Then I spot a single bison, downslope, bulldozing snow. He looks unaware of me so I squat and begin photographing him. When I start to stand again, I hear commotion behind me. Half erect, I turn and come face-to-face with a dozen bison that must have arrived while I was focused on photographing the elk and the single bison. The herd is just twenty yards away, trotting and walking across my return path. Fear fires adrenaline; bison are unpredictable, especially when surprised as these were by my rising from the sagebrush like a predator.

Three of the bison—and this close they are huge—line up at the rear of the herd, looking straight at me, tails raised, a triumvirate of trouble. A raised tail, the saying goes, signifies charge or discharge. And it's doubtful that all three have to discharge at the same time. I reach to the belt of my backpack where I carry my bear spray. It's not there. Damn, I must have left it in the cabin. Too bad; the pepper spray, a trainer said last week, can deter a charging bison.

I can't outrun them; they're five times faster than I am, though they weigh ten times more. My only option is to stand my ground and see if they will accept me and calm down. And maybe I'll calm down, too.

While waiting, my fight or flight response starts to wane. So does that of the bison; one by one the trio's tails drop. Breathing a little easier, I take a few photographs, hoping to capture this intimate moment with wild creatures. Then I slowly walk away and upslope, hoping to circle behind them and back to the ranch. When I reach the ridgeline above them and look down, two of the triumvirate are bulldozing; the third follows my every move. He and I share one long last look before I start down the other side of the ridge, out of his view.

Moving downslope, I repeatedly glance back, scanning for danger, like the elk did with me. The metal crampons of my snowshoes clatter against rocks—more glacial debris—lurking beneath a thin layer of wind-swept snow. After I cross the herd's tracks, the downhill grade grows steeper, the snow deeper. I'm half walking, half falling onto all fours, my legs and hands flailing against sagebrush, filling the air with its sweet menthol.

I stop, bend down, break off a twig, rub the sage on my mustache, and inhale deeply. The aroma soothes. I gaze upslope to where endless blue meets a ridge of white. At last I've sensed this valley and my place in it. I'm excited, a bit scared, and brimming with joy that I've found just what I sought on my day off.

3

How Death Feeds Life

———

A couple weeks later, just after work, Mary and I start our dinner simmering and slip out of the bunkhouse kitchen and onto the back porch. Earlier today, one of the instructors stopped by the ranch to tell us that he had just spotted a bison calf lying in the snow, and it didn't look well. He had watched it raise its head, try to stand up, and fall back down. The calf is just across the main road from the ranch, close enough that from this back porch we should be able to see it with our naked eyes as well as zero in with a spotting scope.

I set up a scope, locate the calf, and zoom in on blood that dots the snow near its head, as if sprayed by a cough or sneeze. The instructor didn't know what had happened to the animal. I wonder if it has internal injuries after being hit by a visitor's car. The calf is so still that it looks dead, until the head rises a couple of inches and then flops back onto the snow.

There are no predators or scavengers nearby yet, but when I scan to the west, I discover about a quarter mile away a coyote mingling with a bison herd. Its head is down and its ears are twitching as it listens for a possible snack: mice or voles scurrying beneath the snow after being disturbed by the grazing bison. I step away from the scope so that Mary can take my place.

She swivels the scope and surveys the calf. "Huh," she mutters and zooms the instrument. A moment later she says, "I think I see coyote tracks." She looks at me and adds, "This could get interesting."

When Mary and I return to the kitchen, we dish up our dinner and sit at the dining room table with the two other volunteers, Karen and George. There are no seminars for a couple of days so the four of us have the bunkhouse to ourselves. I chatter on about how excited I am to watch what will happen to the calf. It could feed many other animals—could even draw a wolf pack. I want to observe and understand how the food web develops, how death feeds life.

Without taking his eyes off his soup, George says in a soft voice, "I don't think it's right."

I stop a forkful of noodles halfway to my mouth and ask, "What's not right?"

He stares at me. "Watching the calf die."

"Why not?"

He puts his spoon down and rubs a hand over his head, which he shaved recently in support of his nephew who has lost his hair during chemotherapy. "It feels disrespectful to me. Like you're spying."

"Oh, come on, George. That calf will die whether I watch or not. And I can't believe that it knows I'm a quarter mile away and staring through a spotting scope."

He studies his bowl of soup and says, "I'd rather not hear any more about it."

There's a chilly silence until Karen changes the subject, and we finish eating in peace.

Peace is important. Though George has his own cabin and Karen has hers, we volunteers eat and work together every day. Friction could make the winter feel very long.

Early the next morning, when I return to the back porch alone and stand near the scope, I'm thinking about George's comments—and feeling guilty. Was he right: Am I a voyeur? I'm also wondering if the calf died overnight when the temperature fell to fifteen degrees. I can't imagine how it survived both the cold and its injury.

Curiosity overcomes guilt, and I scan with my naked eyes. A herd of about forty bison grazes within a hundred yards of the calf but ignores it. I push away more guilt and peer into the scope. The calf is not moving. But a few moments later, the calf raises its head just off the snow and then lays it back down.

I step from the scope and consider the situation. I'm not driving a bus today, so I'll be here cleaning. There is no field seminar and no participants are staying at the ranch. Mary will be in and out much of the day and everyone else will be gone. It's just me, this calf, and whatever is going to happen. This could be the first time I see who benefits from an animal's death and how they do so, the first time to try to take a naturalist's viewpoint. And that is a big part of why I chose to volunteer in Yellowstone.

I first visited this park more than thirty years ago. I was a tourist, and Yellowstone was another spot to highlight in my dog-eared road atlas. Twenty-five years later, Mary and I returned and fell in love with this place. I was hooked and longed to learn more about this rare and fragile, wild and complete ecosystem.

More summers passed with more trips to bike, backpack, and canoe in Yellowstone. I learned something new every time and that whet my appetite for more. After we retired, Mary and I were accepted as winter volunteers. I arrived primed to immerse myself in this valley, to understand its ecology, how its plants and animals fit together. This calf presents a perfect opportunity to do just that.

Regardless of George's objections and my conflicting feelings, I will scope this scene every hour or so and take notes with a digital voice recorder. But, for George's sake, I'll keep what I see to myself.

Two hours later I'm back at the scope with Mary, who just popped in and will soon pop out. We are surprised to discover that the calf has moved from one side of a willow bush to the other. Where the calf once lay, a couple of ravens waddle around, a comical sight even though they're pecking at blood-stained snow. A big cow, probably the calf's mother, plods over from where she was grazing. She licks the calf's side; its body twitches and its head shakes. The few early-bird photographers who have discovered this roadside photo opportunity hunch over tripod-mounted cameras that sport expensive telephoto lenses.

Mary has her eye to a second scope and grumbles, "They're too close to that calf."

As I watch, a photographer with a lens as long as his arm and as big around as his head creeps even closer. "That lens is so powerful that he could just as easily back away and still get great shots," I say with contempt.

"Yeah, but he wants the money shot," Mary replies.

This winter we have both spent numerous days driving groups of photographers in search of wildlife. We have heard them challenge each other about taking the "money shot," a picture so good that they can sell it or hang it proudly, like a trophy.

An hour later I am back at the scope by myself. The word is out; fourteen photographers now crowd the roadside in a feeding frenzy as the mom returns to the calf and nudges it with her big head. Though I can't hear from this distance, I bet she is making the low grunts that cows use to signal distress or locate a calf. With each nudge, the calf's body quivers, but the head doesn't move. Nine months ago, this calf walked and suckled within a few hours of birth. As it fed, its mother licked it, and her scent and touch must have filled the calf's new world. Now, as the calf slips from this world, that scent and touch must comfort again.

The mom swings her head toward the road and stares in the direction of the photographers. Bison have poor vision; she probably can't see them, but she can hear and smell them. She turns back to the calf and nudges it again, careful not to poke it with her horns. The calf's mouth and nose are partially buried in the snow; breathing must be difficult.

The mom leaves and begins grazing a few yards away, head toward the photographers, obviously aware of them. I imagine her charging and the photographers running for the protection of their cars and I chuckle. I widen the scope's field of vision to encircle mom and calf. Does she feel sad? Does the calf feel fear? I have read that once a bison cow senses she cannot save her calf—say, from an attacking grizzly—she will walk away. This is a matter of efficiency; half of all calves do not survive past their third winter. But a cow must save her energy to breed again; the herd's survival depends on it.

Still, no predators or scavengers are near the calf, other than the photographers who keep inching closer. As soon as one moves forward, another follows suit. I have found that photographers are like ravens: They'll find a kill anywhere. Ravens are so skilled at kill finding that some experts believe that hungry wolves travel to where they see ravens soaring and circling. Wolves would do well to watch photographers, too.

At lunchtime I leave my mop and bucket and return hesitantly to the bunkhouse and onto the back porch. I take a deep breath and look into the scope. The calf is so flat that it looks boneless. A single coyote, attentive and cautious, and judging from its size a male, stands about a yard from the calf's hindquarters. The coyote skulks forward, sniffing, tail down. The calf twitches, and the coyote jumps back. A moment later he slinks closer, pokes the calf with his right front paw. The calf shudders, the coyote leaps. This dance continues; the calf struggling to maintain its life, the coyote working to sustain his. The mom grazes a hundred yards away. Is she even aware of the danger to her calf?

The coyote moves in and ducks his head out of my view and into the tender—and vulnerable—underbelly near the calf's rear legs. When he comes back into view, he has a mouth full of fur. I gasp. He dives back in and reappears with more fur. Eventually he's going to come up with hide and blood. Do I want to watch anymore?

I look around without the scope. There are at least twenty photographers now, the newest arrivals frantically erecting tripods in the road, right in the way of traffic. It hardly matters; visitors are stopping cars anywhere and everywhere, compelled to watch as the coyote stands atop the calf.

I also can't resist and return to the scope. The coyote looks like a dog with a pull toy: head low, canine teeth hooked into hide, front and rear legs stretched forward, back arched. While pulling, he repeatedly and violently twists his head from side to side. Even through the scope I can feel his power. The calf wriggles but cannot escape. The coyote is trying to eat the calf while it's still alive. This makes sense; once the animal dies, the meat will freeze. This meal will never be warmer, softer, or easier. But understanding the efficiency of this doesn't make it any less gruesome to observe.

I step away from the scope, look down, and study the gray porch floor, its paint chipped here and there. I close my eyes, put a palm to each cheek, shake my head and grunt. I open my eyes, look at the scope but not into it. I turn and stare at the door to the kitchen. Remembering my desire to see the food web in action, I curse and step back to the scope.

No blood stains the coyote's muzzle, so he hasn't broken through yet. The calf raises its head and looks back at the predator. The coyote does not move away; he just glances toward the calf's eyes and then at where he will bite next. The calf's head falls back to the snow, and a large cloud of breath, perhaps its last, rises into the cold air, soft and white against the dark fur. I release a long, sad sigh.

The coyote stops, turns, looks toward the photographers, and starts circling the calf. He stares into the calf's eyes, and then saunters along the backbone to the rump. He pokes the calf, but it doesn't move. He pushes his muzzle against the calf. Still no movement. He yawns, looks almost bored. Perhaps he knows that the animal is dead and that there's no danger here, just a fine feast. There's no competition in sight, the sun is out, and the day is relatively warm—about 25 degrees. The coyote curls up in the snow.

I leave the scope; I don't need to watch this dog sleep. Instead, I go into the bunkhouse to have my lunch and escape the scene. Eating alone, I spend the mealtime lost in conflicting thoughts, feelings, and images about life, death, and watching an animal die.

After finishing a sandwich and convincing myself that observing how death feeds life is important, I return to the porch. The calf's mom is grazing a hundred yards away. Seventeen photographers zoom and focus and compose. The coyote is at the soft underbelly; his bloody muzzle shocks me. It took an hour, but he is finally in. I leave the porch, wondering if I'll continue watching now that blood has been drawn.

When I resume my watch later, the coyote is gone and so are most of the photographers. A raven sits in the snow far from the calf and appears to be eating. Perhaps, while I was away, the coyote ripped off a piece of meat and walked away with it, dropping scraps. As the calf gets spread around the landscape, the food web will widen; scavengers—especially ravens—will join the feast.

Scientists have found that ravens arrive at a kill within minutes, sometimes even before the kill. Their beaks are not made for opening a carcass; they need coyotes—or wolves—to do that. They eat side by side with the dogs, often chased away but rarely harmed. They also fly off with bits of meat, cache this stash, and return for more. Scientists calculate that because of this caching, ravens actually get more meat from the kill than the wolves. Some believe that one reason wolves hunt in packs is so that they can consume more of a kill before ravens airlift it away.

Meat dangling from its beak, the raven flies off as two coyotes approach. I recognize them: a big male and a female, her tail ratty from mange. They are a mating pair and have claimed this part of the valley as their territory. They stop and lie down in the snow some distance from the carcass. They are attentive to the remaining photographers and show no sign of moving in on the meal.

When I next return to my vigil, a full day of observation has passed since I first spotted the calf. I lean against the kitchen door frame and look unaided across the road. A row of a dozen photographers still dines on the drama. Several chat like they're at a parade, voices drifting over to me on the breeze. The entire bison herd, with the mom on the fringe, lies about seventy yards away from the carcass. While I'd like to think they are paying their respects, this is more likely what's called "loafing," a mundane step in their digestive process.

I hear coyotes yelping from Ranger Hill, just beside the bunkhouse. I zoom the scope in on the mating pair near the carcass and wait for their reaction. They throw their heads back; their breath escapes without sound. Two seconds later their howls reach me. The Ranger Hill coyotes reply. I'm in the middle of a canine call and response. I smile and applaud silently.

When I return two hours later, only ravens and magpies are feeding. One raven sits on the head and pecks at the calf's eye. A bald eagle rests on a rock nearby, waiting its turn, though it dwarfs the other birds and could easily kill and eat them. One expert calls our national bird a shy scavenger, and from what I've seen, the name fits.

Now, as the ravens dine, the single coyote that first opened the carcass stands forty yards away, surveying them. He approaches cautiously, ears perked. The ravens and magpies depart; the eagle keeps its distance. The coyote sniffs around, pulls off a chunk of meat and drags it away, blood staining the snow.

For the first time, I have no emotional reaction. I have stopped looking at the calf and seeing suffering. Now I look at a carcass and see sustenance. I've stopped viewing this as a conflicted tourist. Instead, I'm starting to analyze this as an objective naturalist.

When I next step onto the porch Mary is again with me. The smell of pasta sauce follows us out the kitchen door, spices the air, and drifts away. I scan the scene: Clouds have formed, the temperature has dropped, and snow is falling. Perhaps this is what chased away all the photographers, or maybe they're at dinner too. The bison herd is still far from the carcass, but two bison now bookend it. I can't tell if either is the mom.

I look into the scope and zoom in on the male of the coyote mating pair. He is eating and bloodied to his ears. He stops, walks away, bows down, and wipes either side of his face in the snow, painting bloody swaths. He finishes his after-dinner ablutions by driving his muzzle into snow up to his eyes. Then he rejoins his ratty-tailed mate. After some sniffing and snuggling, they return to the carcass and alternate short bursts of eating and peering into the fading daylight. A few moments later, the Ranger Hill coyotes yelp, and I understand the pair's caution. I can't see the yelpers but can distinguish several voices.

Mary, watching through another scope that is pointed toward Ranger Hill and the yelping, whispers with awe, "I think there's a wolf coming down the hill."

We hold our breath as two indistinct shapes move down Ranger Hill and in the direction of the bunkhouse. If they are wolves, they are higher on the pecking order and will run the coyotes off. Finally, they're close enough that we can tell they are coyotes.

"I'll bet those are the ones we heard yelping a minute ago," I say.

"Whoa! Look at that. Raised leg urination!" Mary exclaims. Both newcomers from Ranger Hill have raised a leg, urinated, and kicked snow on it. Only alphas—male and female—raise their legs to urinate; all other pack members squat. This alpha pair is marking territory already claimed by the mating pair that's dining across the road. Trouble is brewing. The Ranger Hill coyotes move toward the road then back up the slope then back to the road, the line that separates them from a fight and a meal.

"Looks like they're trying to decide whether to challenge the other coyotes," I say, as a bull bison, huge in comparison, saunters right by the Ranger Hill coyotes.

As the Ranger Hill coyotes tussle with one another, Mary says, "I think they're egging each other on."

Finally, they cross the road and begin loping toward the carcass. The lope becomes a sprint. When they reach the mating pair, they slow down, lower their heads, bare their canines, tuck tails between their legs, and arch their backs.

"Alligator!" Mary yells, calling this dominance move by its coyote-watcher name.

One of the Ranger Hill coyotes chases the male of the mating pair. As they race away from the carcass, the Ranger Hill coyote bites the male's rump. The male is the picture of fear: running full out, tail between his legs, mouth wide open, and head turned toward his pursuer.

Meanwhile, back at the carcass, the ratty-tailed female of the mating pair has strolled ten yards away and is nonchalantly washing her face and peacefully granting the carcass to the second Ranger Hill coyote.

Some of Yellowstone's wildlife biologists believe that because the Lamar Valley is so small the animals that live here know one another. If this is true, it's possible that the Ranger Hill coyotes knew that the male of the mating pair wouldn't leave without a squabble. And that his mate was not real competition and could be allowed to stroll.

The Ranger Hill coyote quits the chase and trots back to the carcass, head high. He joins his partner in their prize. The vanquished male sits and starts cleaning himself.

I move the scope around and spot the single coyote that discovered and opened the calf. From a safe distance, he is watching the two pairs battle for what was once his meal. All five coyotes look healthy. This fits what a veteran wolf watcher told me: Since wolf reintroduction in 1995, only smart and strong coyotes have survived.

The last sight I see before darkness draws a curtain across the scene is the Ranger Hill coyotes ravaging the carcass. Mary and I also head into dinner. I long to describe to George and Karen the turf battle and alligators we just witnessed. I want to share my detailed observations of who ate what. But for George's sake I keep my mouth shut.

During the night, through our open cabin window, Mary and I hear more coyote howling than we have heard all winter. In the dark, we whisper and wonder if this is due to the carcass and a turf war.

Early the next morning the resident ranger, Brian, moves the carcass another quarter mile from the road to reduce the danger to the pack of photographers. They are so focused on the money shot, one could easily step into the road and be hit by the car of a driver who is just as distracted.

Then Brian stops by the bunkhouse and says that this calf was born nine months ago. It would have been gaining about forty pounds a month and probably weighs more than three hundred pounds. That's a nice meal for five coyotes, a flock of ravens, some magpies, and a shy bald eagle.

Two days after I started observing the calf, I step to the scope and study the remains: ribs and backbone, stripped of meat and bright red. The hide lies on the snow, a rumpled rug. I count fifteen ravens, some calling to each other, and three magpies. Two coyotes stand at opposite ends of the remains, until one runs the other off with the alligator move. Only two photographers brave the cold wind blowing in from the southwest. The rest of their pack has moved on, hungry for other shots.

Later, just after dinner, when I check the scope for the last time, the only creature left is a single magpie. I walk away from the scope, down the steps, and along the ranch's snow-covered driveway that winds toward the main road. Each step away from the scope relieves me.

Though we've backpacked for years deep in Yellowstone's backcountry, I've had a tourist's view of wildlife framed by spectacular scenery. I've detoured around bison, run from a charging moose family, and backed down from an ornery elk. I've marveled at a racing antelope, watched a bold coyote walk right through a line of photographers, and been spellbound by a wolf pack trotting along a sunlit ridge.

But until now I had never forced myself to watch the bloody death and life battle as prey fights death and predator struggles to survive. I had never observed from a naturalist's point of view, never witnessed firsthand how death feeds life.

I'm glad the first time is over. I hope it's not the last.

4

You Just Can't Keep a Good Coyote Down

———

Yellowstone's coyotes had no idea who the new dog in the neighborhood was when wolves were reintroduced in the park after a seventy-year absence. Generations of coyotes had come and gone without a wolf in sight. But coyotes soon learned that these new dogs sure could bring down elk. The reintroduced wolves, on the other hand, knew exactly who the coyotes were: competitors for hard-won food.

A Yellowstone coyote is a medium-sized dog, like a Border Collie. A wolf, on the other hand, is a giant dog, like a Great Dane. Wolves are a foot taller at the shoulder and weigh four times as much as coyotes.

So when a hungry—and naive—coyote sidled up to join wolves at their kill, the wolf pack did what it does best: cut the competition by one competitor at a time, whether that rival is a wolf from another pack, a fox, a mountain lion, or a coyote. (Wolves rarely eat the competitors they kill.)

Within a few years after wolf reintroduction, the Lamar Valley coyote population had been reduced by half. Yet today, there are as many coyotes in the valley as there were before the wolves returned. That's an impressive recovery, but I wouldn't expect less from the coyote, an intelligent, tough survivor with a long history of overcoming adversity inside and outside the park.

When Yellowstone, the world's first park, was established in 1872, no one had experience managing a park or protecting its wildlife. Protecting wildlife wasn't even a high priority. Yellowstone was created to preserve the area's magnificent scenery and magical geothermal features; the animals just happened to live within the new boundary lines. And anyway, there was no money to hire staff to safeguard wildlife. So, for example, miners passing through the Lamar Valley on their way to claims near Cooke City hunted wolves and coyotes for sport or profit.

By the time wildlife protection was considered, park officials were only thinking about protecting bison, elk, deer, bighorn sheep, and antelope from predators. To their minds, *protecting* wildlife meant *killing* wolves and coyotes.

In 1896 coyote control was recommended, and poisoned animal carcasses were the weapon of choice. Eight years later with the coyotes still holding their own, the park superintendent wrote in his annual report that he needed to escalate the war. He vowed to use "every means to get rid of them." Three years after that, the war ratcheted up another notch when the U.S. army, which had been put in charge of the park, deployed soldiers against coyotes.

This war against predators did not go unnoticed. By the late 1920s, people inside and outside the National Park

Service—the group next in charge—were questioning the heavy-handed destruction of wolves and coyotes. Scientific organizations were speaking out against predator control, saying that these animals helped maintain ecological balance. The view that predators were necessary and should be protected became NPS policy in 1936, and the sanctioned killing of wolves and coyotes in Yellowstone stopped.

In the forty years between poisoning the first carcass and firing the last shot, more than 4,300 Yellowstone coyotes were killed. But that did not drive them from the park. In contrast, it only took seven years to kill 132 wolves and eradicate them from the park.

How could the little coyote survive a battle that the big bad wolf could not?

Coyotes are opportunistic feeders; they'll eat just about anything that doesn't move or moves more slowly than they do. In 1937 Adolf Murie and his assistants conducted a landmark study of coyotes in the Lamar Valley. They scoured the valley floor, picked up more than 5,000 pieces of coyote scat, and analyzed them. They found that coyotes ate twelve kinds of large mammals; twenty-four different small mammals; twenty types of birds, fish, and snakes; four kinds of bugs; as well as grass, pine nuts, rose seeds, strawberries, mushrooms, blueberries, and Oregon grape. (That's more varied than the fare Mary and I have all winter at the ranch!) They also found in the scat remnants of leather work gloves, twine, cellophane, tinfoil, and shoestrings.

Such a varied diet makes poisoning coyotes more difficult than poisoning wolves, which prefer a single-item menu: elk.

Poison the right elk carcass and you could kill an entire wolf pack.

Also, the size of the dog and its pack matters. The small coyote presents a more challenging target to a bounty hunter with a rifle. And when hunted by humans, coyotes decrease the size of their packs; smaller packs are less obvious and harder to track. Wolves, on the other hand, rarely travel alone and always live in packs; the larger the pack the better, from the wolf's point of view. And from the view of a hunter who is paid by the pelt.

Perhaps most important, unlike wolves, coyote reproduction is "density dependent." If hunters and trappers kill many coyotes in a particular area, the surviving coyotes will produce *more* young than usual. According to one study, a coyote population can withstand an annual loss of seventy percent and still generate enough young to replace that loss.

These differences between the two animals are why predator control led to an *increase* in Yellowstone's coyote population and the eradication of wolves. The story was the same beyond the park's boundaries where hunters and trappers paid with government funds destroyed the predators.

Among those paid hunters was a predator control agent in New Mexico in the early 1920s named Aldo Leopold. He was good at his job and helped cut that state's wolf population from 300 to 30 in just three years. When he saw the light about killing predators, it came as a fading green fire in the eyes of a wolf he had just shot. He wrote an essay about that experience and it was published in a book in 1949, shortly after Leopold's death. That book, *A Sand County Almanac*, would become one of the most significant environmental books of the 20th century.

Leopold's new ideas—including his 1944 recommendation to bring wolves back to Yellowstone—would lead to the development of environmental ethics and wilderness conservation. But that would take decades. Meanwhile, the killing of predators continued.

By the 1970s, the range of the wolf, which had once covered over two-thirds of the United States, had shrunk to include just Alaska, northern Michigan, northern Wisconsin, and northern Minnesota.

Coyotes—those tough little survivors—fared better than wolves in the predator war outside Yellowstone just as they had in the park, despite federal, state, and private hunters resorting to a gruesome arsenal. Hunters used snares, steel traps, and long-range rifles. They engaged in chemical warfare: anti-fertility chemicals, cyanide, sugar-coated strychnine, and other poisons. They used biological warfare: introducing mange so that coyotes would lose fur and die during winter. They flooded dens or set them on fire, hunted from airplanes and snowmobiles.

All of this against a critter the size of a Border Collie.

And when the dust settled, coyotes, which before the onslaught had been concentrated in the Great Plains, now lived in every state except Hawaii. They have even taken up residence in large cities like Chicago, Washington, D.C., and Los Angeles, where packs have learned to avoid humans by hunting at night and not howling.

Yep, you just can't keep a good coyote down.

5

Vanity at Trout Lake

———

I'm alone and heading for Trout Lake to find my place, sit in quiet, and see what wildlife appears. Daylight is arriving and a light snow is falling. One hundred yards from the parking lot I come to a big bull bison, lying across the trail, his back collecting snow like a well-insulated roof. He stares at me with old brown eyes that deliver a clear message: *I'm not moving.*

In Yellowstone, bison are "25-yard animals." That's the space visitors are required to give them. For good reason. Bison are wild, fast, and unpredictable; they are not just big cattle. This old bull could be up and on me before I could make a clumsy snowshoe turn and try to run. Or he could lie here all day. I can't fathom what he's thinking.

But I can think about my options. The trail is crowded on one side by a steep slope and on the other by trees. I can't sneak past the bull and maintain that safety cushion. I can head back to my van or take another route to the lake, though this is the only trail.

I am on this trail because MacNeil Lyons, a Yellowstone instructor and photographer, inspired me yet again when he spoke last night about how he finds and photographs wildlife. The key, he said, is moving in silence and sitting with patience. I decided right then to return to Trout Lake for a second time. The first visit was with MacNeil two years ago.

It was a Christmas holiday and Mary and I were finishing four days as participants in our first wildlife-watching seminar. MacNeil, the instructor, led all ten participants along the trail to Trout Lake, where he asked us to form a circle and take turns sharing what those four days had meant to each of us. Two people wept with joy as they spoke. Then MacNeil delivered an inspiring sermon on the importance of wildness. He closed by reciting a poem, and I'll never forget him standing there, sunlit on a snowy ridge above the lake, eyes closed, enraptured by the wild.

That moment inspired Mary and me to return for other seminars and eventually apply to volunteer. Now we help MacNeil and other instructors deliver seminars like those we attended. We are in the perfect place to experience the wildness of which MacNeil spoke.

So maybe this bison is a sign that I should take a wilder route, avoid the trail altogether, bushwhack to the lake. Maybe I'll find more wildlife that way. Maybe that's what MacNeil would do. And—it's difficult being this honest—I would love to be more like MacNeil.

I nod to the bison and start bushwhacking up the steep slope through virgin snow. I'm postholing—sinking knee-deep into the powder—and soon panting. Sage abounds and every time I brush the uncovered branches, its sweet, pungent aroma refreshes me.

I reach an old snowshoe trail almost refilled by recent snowfall but still packed underneath. I follow the trail upslope until it disappears, and I'm postholing again.

When the slope gets even steeper, I take a lesson from animals that I have watched this winter and drop onto all fours. Though climbing is easier, and I'd be embarrassed if anyone saw me, efficiency trumps vanity, and I crawl upward.

At the top of the slope, I stand and survey the area. Ahead, the grade levels for a bit before there's another ridge to climb. Behind, I see the snow-covered road. Across from the road, a high ridgeline appears miragelike through a shroud of snow. Although I don't know exactly where the lake is now that I'm off trail, the road and the ridgeline are good landmarks for the return trip. I should be able to find my way back. It's only a mile, for heaven's sake.

Two slopes later, I stop, wipe sweat from my eyes, and mutter a few curse words. I'm certain the trail along which we followed MacNeil on that memorable day was not this difficult. Maybe bushwhacking isn't a good idea. Maybe I should turn around. What would MacNeil do?

Since he's been exploring Yellowstone for a decade and has led many groups to the lake, I assume he would have an idea of where he was. If not, he would at the least have a compass and a map. Oh, I have a compass, one I've used with success for wilderness route finding. It's in the glove compartment of the van at the trailhead. And I have a map, too, neatly stored in our cabin. I forgot both this morning in my rush into the wild.

And I have reached the wild; there's not a trail—except mine—visible anywhere, just smooth snow under flocked conifers. Swaying trees creak against each other; falling snow murmurs as it drops onto my hood; the call of an unseen raven reverberates. I gaze upslope to where conifers end and sky begins. Maybe I'll see the lake from there, and I won't have to return to the ranch, tail between my legs, having failed to reach my goal.

After still more postholing, I reach the crest and there below me is the lake and the distinctive footbridge across its outlet creek. I snowshoe to the middle of the footbridge. The creek below it roars under a cover of ice and snow.

I made it! And for the first time since leaving the trail, I know where I am. Relief and pride flow through me as sweat trickles down my back. I shake through an uncoordinated little victory dance. Then I look around for a place where I can sit quietly and patiently—like MacNeil.

But before I can find that place, the snowfall that's been light all morning intensifies. Dumbfounded, I watch as the trees across the lake—about a quarter mile away—disappear from view. This is not good. I'm tired, cold, and unsure where the actual trail is. Heavier snowfall will increase the difficulty of trail finding, seeing the landmark ridgeline, and hearing road noise. This is a recipe for getting lost.

Common sense wins out. I'm not going to sit here like MacNeil. No way! I'm retreating to the van right now. And I'm going to take the real trail—the easier route, bull bison or no bull bison.

Determined and anxious, I step from the bridge onto the obvious trail that winds through the forest. This should lead to the main trail. With little snow on the ground under these thick trees, I move along with ease. Until the trail starts to veer to the right, the opposite direction from the way I want. Damn! Somehow I missed the main trail.

Decision time. I can keep following this path, but it's turning away from the road and the van. I can backtrack and try to find the main trail. I can bushwhack from here and hope for a shortcut.

The climbing and postholing to get this far have beaten me down; I don't want to go in the opposite direction or backtrack. Forget options one and two. But the snow's falling heavier by the minute, cutting visibility further, and making the third option dicey. I stop and tell myself—a literal muttering to the trees—"As long as I go generally downhill, I'll hit the road. If I can't see the parking lot, I'll just have to guess where it is." I shrug my shoulders and bushwhack away.

As I leave the forest and wade into much deeper snow, the wind smears snow across my glasses. Everything appears squiggly, but I don't want to waste time wiping them. Besides, every few steps I fall over and get them snowy again. Swimming in and rising from the deep snow is tiring. I yell at myself for not bringing trekking poles. They would make getting up so much easier, might even stop me from falling. But I wanted to leave my hands free for capturing MacNeil-like pictures of wildlife. Who was I kidding?

After a few more falls, I notice that I always topple to my left. Lying once again in the deep snow, feeling my heart pound and energy drain, I curse the snow. Why will it support my right foot but not my left?

I struggle back up, brush off now-wet gloves, and trudge forward. Until I fall again. This time I denounce myself, shouting that I'm too damned old for this. I don't ask what MacNeil would do; he's half my age and wouldn't allow himself to be caught in this predicament. My heart's frantic pounding scares me. How much more can it take? I wrestle myself upright.

With the next fall, I rest in the snow waiting for my gasping to subside, even though I feel chilling moisture soaking into my pants. Finally, I use what seems like the last of my energy to get up. Within a few steps, I reach snow that supports me. Relieved, I make good time in a direction that I hope leads to the road. But I'm wobbly and feel out of sorts. Am I tired, dehydrated, or just too old?

I come to a steep slope and decide to slide down it on my rear—anything to make this easier and quicker. I sit down, lean back, raise both feet well out of the snow, and push off. Fatigue and uncertainty vanish, and for a moment I'm sleigh-riding like a kid. I even let out a joyous whoop before I plow into the snow at the bottom.

After I slide and whoop down another ridge and walk out from behind a little hill, I hear the diesel rattle of a speeding pickup truck. The road! I stop and laugh. I made it! And what a great story I have to tell. Then I look down at my feet. And do a double take. I'm wearing only one snowshoe!

All at once, the staggering and falling makes perfect sense. I must have lost my left snowshoe before I started falling down. Back there. About a mile back there. Up two steep slopes. Unbelievable!

I look at the road and then behind me. I'm soaked and starting to shiver, but I face two big decisions. The first is whether to tell anyone about this. Ever. How could I walk for almost a mile without a snowshoe? Why didn't I figure this out, when I always fell to the left? How could I not notice the snowshoe missing when I slid down two slopes with both feet way up in the air in front of me? My ego shrinks just thinking about it.

The second decision is whether I'm willing to slog back to where I lost the snowshoe. Up those two steep slopes, through that postholing-deep snow, maybe all the way back to the lake.

But if I don't retrieve that snowshoe, I'll have to answer the embarrassing question from Mary and my other adventure partners, "How could you lose a snowshoe?"

Vanity prevails. I turn around and start retracing my steps. I pretend that I'm a search-and-rescue guy tracking an idiot wearing only one snowshoe. His tracks are obvious: snowshoe on the right foot, boot on the left. He must be deranged. People like that shouldn't be allowed in the wild.

I claw my way up the two slopes. I reach the deep snow where I struggled. The places where I fell are obvious—little bomb craters—and I search each one.

In time, after much huffing and puffing, I see the lake. And there, under a conifer in the middle of the trail, in an area almost devoid of snow, sits my snowshoe. Mocking me. It's right-side up and looks like a display in a store window. I pick it up and inspect it. I can't force my boot into it without loosening the straps. But somehow my boot had slipped out. Without my knowing it. And I had just walked away.

I sit down and strap on the snowshoe. I tighten it and try to kick it off. Not possible. I snug up my other snowshoe and gulp some water. I start walking—for the third time— through the deep snow. By now, I've made a wide trail that even I can follow since the single snowshoe packed down the trail's right side on the way to the road and its left side on the way back.

At last I reach the road but the parking lot is nowhere to be seen. I guess that I'm a half-mile west of the van. I long to stroll down the road's hard-packed snow and ice. But to reach it, I have to get over the roadside berm made by weeks of snowplowing; it's taller than I am. I start up the berm and sink to my crotch.

Standing there, feeling trapped, I again drop down on all fours and inch myself to the top of the berm. A car goes by; faces pressed against windows stare. I don't care; desperation has driven out vanity, I'm immune to embarrassment—all I want is to get in the van, out of these wet clothes, and in front of the heater.

When I reach the van, its thermometer reads twenty-two degrees. I climb into the back and strip; every layer of clothing is soaked. I change into spare clothes, curl up in front of the blasting heater, and recall the morning. Decisions based on pride and vanity led me to flounder around in the wild for almost four hours. And in all that time, I knew where I was for a measly fifteen minutes. I didn't sit quiet and patient like MacNeil. I didn't take a single photo.

I didn't see any animals except the old bison that I interpreted as a sign to take the wilder route. Maybe I read that sign wrong. Maybe that old bison was a reminder that I should pay attention to my age. Maybe his lying there signaled that I should take the easier route, which would have been to come back another day when he was elsewhere. But instead, I bushwhacked without map or compass, at times wondering whether my body could take anymore.

Sitting in the van safe, sound, and starting to warm, I stare through the windshield at the wild and snowy landscape. I realize just how lucky I was and say aloud, "What was I thinking?" No answer comes.

I'm going to have to work on my MacNeilness. I'll have to ask him for a private lesson in quiet and patience. And wilderness decision-making. Then, I'll stealthily watch how he keeps his snowshoes on.

6

Cottonwoods and Sage, Elk and Wolves

Just past the first of the six tall cottonwoods in this stand, I stop walking and kneel by Rose Creek. My knees settle into the snow's cold softness. Though it is mid-February, the creek is still running, but ice clings to the tops of the rocks that protrude above the moving water. I take off my gloves and tap some clinging ice. It crumbles to kernels which fall from the rock and drift downstream, twirling and twinkling in the morning sun until they disappear around a bend, seeking the Lamar River.

I take off my glasses, slide them into a pocket, and dip a cupped hand into the creek. I splash a handful of winter-cold water onto my face and groan with pain and pleasure. Drops trickle down my cheeks and through my mustache, and I taste the creek. I rub my chilled hand over my face and feel the warmth of friction and the joy of this communion.

I stand, put on my glasses, and look around. A short distance to the north is the road that runs the length of the Lamar Valley. When I drive a bus filled with participants and an instructor along that road—as I did during the three days since my Trout Lake fiasco—I'm surrounded by others hungry for knowledge and experts happy to provide it. That is a dream come true, and I can't think of a better way to learn about this valley.

But there is a different way: finding a place near the ranch that I can walk to regularly and know intimately by watching, listening, touching, smelling, and tasting. A small place where I hope that something as simple as learning about one tree can generate questions that lead me to better understand the ecology of this valley, maybe even the ecology of Yellowstone. This stand of cottonwoods is the place that I have chosen for that exploration, which began with that Rose Creek communion.

I turn and walk the few paces back to the first cottonwood. This is one of the trees that I admired on my moonlight stroll along the road just three days after we arrived at the ranch. I study the tree in the morning light. Freckles of red lichen adorn its deeply furrowed gray bark. A songbird-sized nest rests in the crotch of a limb high in the tree.

I take from my pack a blue foam pad and place it on the snow beneath the cottonwood. I kneel on the pad and inspect the tree's trunk. Filaments attached to the rough bark wave in the breeze. Each looks like a single light brown strand of hair that the cottonwood plucked from a bison as the animal, trying to remove freeloading insects, scratched against the trunk. I sit on the pad, lean against the tree, rub my back against the bark, smile, and applaud the bison's choice of scratching post.

Cottonwood trees, like people, come in male and female. And, as with people, it takes two to tango. The dance goes like this: The male's flowers contain pollen and each spring the wind whisks that pollen away to fertilize the females. Within a short time, the fertilized females produce pods full of the cottony substance for which the tree is named. Nestled in that cotton are tiny seeds, the hope for cottonwoods' existence. When the pods burst open, the wind catches the cotton, creating what may look like an early summer snowstorm. After the cotton lands along stream banks, the seeds take root and seedlings sprout.

The tree that scratched my back—she's a lady: From the leafless branches above my head, hang a few of her pods, now dried to a red-orange color. Some still contain cotton. Looking at the other trees in the stand, I spot podless males. So the dance happened here and that should mean lots of young cottonwood trees growing nearby—trees taller than seedlings but shorter than these six old trees. But that's not the case.

This stand that I'm getting to know exemplifies a larger problem: in some areas of Yellowstone, cottonwoods are nearly extinct. While wolves were absent from the park, the burgeoning numbers of elk had devoured all the cottonwood seedlings—the next generation of trees—each and every year. Too few wolves led to too many elk and not enough cottonwoods.

I stand, walk away from the cottonwood, and study the snow-covered sagebrush garden filling the valley floor. The tops of sagebrush protrude from the snow for as far as I can see up and down the valley. At my feet, I notice that where sagebrush breaks the surface, the crusted snow has a pattern like fish scales. Where there is no sage, the surface is smooth. Perhaps the prevailing westerly winds sweeping up the valley create this lovely mosaic.

Big Sagebrush (the official name) is a survivor. It can grow where the soil is poor and there is little water. And it survives a long time: plants can live for a hundred years—and still just stand three to six feet tall.

With thumb and forefinger, I grab a couple of tiny gray-green sagebrush leaves. As I rub and squeeze them like a rosary or worry beads, their slick oil greases my fingertips. I bring the leaves to my nose, inhale, and hold my breath, trying to keep their aroma within. Then I exhale until my lungs empty. I repeat this several times, and each time feel more connected to this spot. And to others who have come before me. Native Americans who used these sagebrush vapors for treating colds and headaches could have plucked leaves from this very spot. Sagebrush gardens, like this one, have grown in the same areas of the west for the last several thousand years, unless ranchers removed them—as many did—to make way for non-native cattle fodder.

Besides ranchers, the biggest danger to sagebrush are the ungulates—the elk, deer, and pronghorn—that survive winter on sage's nutritious evergreen leaves and abundant seeds. Sagebrush makes up sixty percent of the elk's winter diet.

To study the impact of these browsing ungulates, scientists built exclosures that surround patches of sagebrush with chain-link fence and keep browsers out. A 1995 study compared the growth of the sagebrush inside and outside the exclosures and found that over a 31-year period, ungulates had overbrowsed the outside sagebrush. The scientists wrote that the ungulate population needed to be controlled and that one way to do this was to bring back wolves. For sagebrush, as with cottonwoods, elk were part of the problem and wolves part of the solution.

So, as I had hoped when I walked to these cottonwoods this morning, intimately experiencing this little spot has led me to a big question: how are cottonwoods and sage, elk and wolves tied together? And like most big ecological questions in Yellowstone, there is more than one answer.

One theory, called Trophic Cascade, goes like this: In the years between the death of the last wolf in 1926 and the reintroduction of the first in 1995, Yellowstone's elk grew lazy. With the wolves gone, they could browse wherever they wanted and for as long as they pleased. Cottonwoods and sage, as well as willows and aspen, suffered. With the wolves back, the theory speculates, those plants should recover.

Two scientists from Oregon State University, Bill Ripple and Bob Beschta, are big promoters of the Trophic Cascade theory. In 1997 Ripple learned that aspen trees in Yellowstone had been declining for years. Others had observed the decline, but no one could agree on its cause. He decided to investigate. He analyzed tree growth, and found that in Yellowstone's aspen groves seedlings had stopped maturing into young trees about the same time that wolves were killed off in the park.

In 2003 Ripple and Beschta studied the trees along the Lamar River and found many tall cottonwoods more than seventy years old—trees that would have been seedlings around the time that the wolves were killed off. They also found thousands of tiny cottonwood seedlings that had grown in the few years since the wolves returned. But they found nothing in between. Beschta told *Science Daily*, "There should also have been hundreds of young trees, but there were none. Long-term elk browsing had been preventing seedlings from getting taller."

With no wolves in the park, the elk dined every year on tender new seedlings. This stopped the cycle of grove regeneration: seedlings growing into young trees that mature and replace dying old trees.

Since the return of wolves, seedlings are again growing into young trees—in certain locations—according to another Ripple and Beschta study. They found cottonwood and willow growing taller each year in sites the scientists labeled as "high risk"—spots where the elk could not see wolves approach or from which the elk had no easy escape route, spots where dining could be deadly. On the other hand, seedlings showed little increase in height at "low-risk" sites—where the elk still felt safe to browse at will. With wolves back, elk were living in what became known as an "ecology of fear" that determined where they browsed.

The Trophic Cascade theory postulates that the benefits of wolf reintroduction do not stop with healthier stands of cottonwoods, willows, aspen, and sagebrush. The benefits cascade deeper into the ecosystem. Where willows are now more abundant, for example, the population of beavers, which feed on willows, has increased. Where more beavers build more dams, streams overflow their banks. The changing waterscape benefits fish, songbirds, insects, and other plants and animals.

I've discussed this Trophic Cascade theory with instructors and scientists who pass through the ranch. Some roll their eyes at the mention of it and say it's too simple a theory for such a complex ecosystem. Some believe that climate change or fire is more of a factor than wolf reintroduction.

I can only imagine the challenge Ripple and Beschta have faced in defending the theory. Ripple's business card shows that he hasn't given up. The front of the card contains all the standard information you would expect. But turn it over and you see two side-by-side pictures. Both images show the same area near the confluence of the Lamar River and Soda Butte Creek. In the center of each picture is an old and much photographed cottonwood. One picture, labeled "Yellowstone Before Wolves," shows only short vegetation around the old cottonwood. The other, labeled "Yellowstone After Wolves," shows the old cottonwood surrounded by head high willows. The difference is striking.

The theory makes sense to me. However, as many people point out, it's too early to say for sure what is behind the changes in Yellowstone's ecosystem. Wolves have been back less than twenty years, not even an eye blink in nature's timetable.

But I have learned one thing for sure today: I have found a little place to become intimate with. By sitting and observing and asking questions, I've come to understand how a cottonwood stand with an uncertain future and some overgrazed sagebrush may be tied to lazy elk and hungry wolves. All that was missing today was a wolf pack hunting elk, and I could have seen every character in this grand ecological drama.

Maybe next time.

7

The Bison's Last Ride

"I think it's a female yearling," Brian, the district ranger, says to the four of us standing across from him. The bison, a sad lump dusted with fresh snow, fills the space at our feet.

I nod toward him but can't take my eyes from the bison calf; she's beautiful, even in death. Short horns reveal her youth. Her brown eyes are still bright and inviting. I remove my glove, reach down, and feel the long hair on her side; its softness surprises me. I run my hand down her thin leg to what looks like a smooth-sided hoof. But the hoof is encircled with tiny ridges, and I, fascinated, run a fingernail over each one. George, Karen, and Mary, squatting and kneeling, are also caressing her. With no discussion, we share a reverent moment, as you would at the bedside of a just-departed loved one.

Though the four of us did not expect to begin our workday like this, when we learned at dawn that Brian needed help, we all wanted in. But first, we had to convince the ranch manager, Bonnie, to let us—all of her staff—go play ranger even though we must clean a dozen cabins, the bunkhouse, and the bathhouse by this afternoon. We pleaded and she relented. Then the four of us paraded toward Brian's cabin, I was light-footed with excitement about getting close to a bison, an animal that we admire every day as we drive buses full of participants in search of wildlife. Brian instructed us to meet him at the bison and to bring the blue sled, which is designed to carry a broken-down snowmobile but used in the park to move dead animals. George and I muscled it into the rear of a bus, the four of us clambered aboard, and I drove us to the bison.

Now, Brian's soft voice interrupts our quiet moment with the calf. "Do you see any evidence of attack by a predator?"

We look at him and shake our heads.

He points to the blood drying around the nose and mouth and says, "That makes me think it was hit by a car."

That's a possibility since the bison was found dead on the road before dawn east of here. Her body would create a traffic hazard, and there will be lots of traffic—today is Friday, the first day of the long President's Weekend. At first light she was dragged for four miles behind a snowplow to this roadside pullout. Now we are going to sled her farther from the road.

George sighs and stands. "What do you think she weighs?"

"Probably about 500 pounds, but," Brian points toward a distant stand of cottonwoods, "it'll get heavier as we pull it out there."

That's our cue to get to work. Brian grasps the front legs; Mary and George take the rear ones. They grunt and lift and roll the bison onto the sled, revealing the side that was dragged along the snow-covered road. The hide isn't damaged, a testament to its toughness. I feel a flat spot on a horn, which is made of material similar to our fingernails, and which the road filed.

Brian asks Karen, Mary, and George to tamp down a three-person-wide path across the valley floor to facilitate our pulling. As they snowshoe away, chatting about what this carcass may attract, I help Brian tie the bison to the sled. He deftly wraps a rope around the rear legs. He resembles a cowboy in a rodeo bulldogging event, so I take out my camera and frame him, the rope, and the legs. The composition intrigues me, and then I'm chagrined: I'm acting just like those pushy photographers that I poked fun at a couple weeks ago as they tried to out-maneuver one another for the money shot of those coyotes eating a dead calf. I silently scold myself and stow the camera. Brian shoots me a quizzical look.

"Is it OK for me to take pictures of this?"

He glances at the bison and then the cottonwoods and gives me an emphatic nod. "Sure. That would be great. Nobody ever gets to see the things rangers do."

Now on assignment, I bend and kneel, twist and turn, happy to be immersed in capturing these images.

When the tampers return, Brian ties one end of a long rope to the front of the sled and throws the rest forward. Lying outstretched in the snow, with short ropes extending at intervals from the main line, it looks like the harness for a dogsled team. Each of the four grabs a short line and slings it over a shoulder.

Before the team can go, Brian pulls a radio from his jacket. He listens, nods, signs off, and says, "That was the Comm Center. They just had a call from two visitors who reported hitting a bison in the dark and snow this morning." He pauses as if delivering a punch line. "They said the bison walked out in the road and hit their truck." He shakes his head and we all laugh. "That's not how it usually happens."

After a couple of months of driving along snowy park roads, we've seen how it probably happened. Calves are always with a herd, and often that herd is walking down the middle of the plowed road, the easiest path in winter. We have all watched cars barge into a herd, impatient drivers rushing to get through. In a situation like that, a spooked animal could swing its head to the side and get clipped by a careless driver. Such waste saddens me.

However death occurred, it's time for the yearling's last trip across the valley floor. I snowshoe in the deep snow alongside the pre-packed trail so I can video the procession. Breath billowing and bent forward, the four haul the sled to the top of a rise. When they head downhill, I notice that the sled picks up speed because of gravity and the lack of anyone braking from behind. The 500-pound sled is gaining on them.

"Look out!" I yell.

Four heads snap around. Each team member jumps to the side. The sled stops right where they had been. We look at one another and then laugh about how difficult it would have been to explain to Bonnie that three of her volunteers were injured by a sleigh-riding bison while the fourth videoed the mishap.

We continue on and about three-quarters of the way to the cottonwoods, just where the trio's pre-packed trail ends, we stop in a low spot from which we can't see the road.

"Maybe we should put her here where the photographers can't see her," George says.

We settle into silence as the reality of our task hits: We are looking for the best place for others to dine on this beautiful, young animal.

Brian looks toward the road and then the cottonwoods. He purses his lips and moves his head from side to side. "Let's go a bit farther."

They drag the sled up another rise, and Brian motions us to stop. "This is a good spot." He turns and points toward the road. "Photographers will be able to shoot it from three different pullouts."

"But how will you keep them from hiking out here for close-ups?" Karen asks.

"We'll cross that bridge when we come to it." After more than twenty years as a Yellowstone ranger, Brian knows how difficult it is to contain photographers. Yet, he still chooses to place the bison so they can photograph wolves and scavengers dining. I'm surprised at the influence photographers hold without knowing it.

We help Brian untie the bison, and on the count of three all of us hoist one side of the sled. The calf flops into the snow. Brian kneels, and the rough sound of his rubbing snow against the sled to remove the calf's blood eclipses any remaining levity that accompanied us here. Unsure what to do now, the four of us stand mute and stare.

At last, George asks Brian, "Can I help?"

Head down, Brian holds out his bloody work glove like a cop stopping traffic. "That's probably not a good idea."

He starts stowing ropes, and the four of us encircle the bison, mourners at a graveside. A bald eagle lands high in the nearby cottonwoods, waiting.

Brian stands, brushes snow from his knees and gloves, and states, "You know, even though this is an unnatural way for the bison to die, it will feed many other animals."

I nod in silence, thankful to be reminded of a way to see some value in this death.

Brian pulls the sled away, and the others snowshoe in silence behind, family following the hearse from the cemetery. I stay and take two final pictures. I walk to the bison's head and gaze into her brown eye, now dull. Snowflakes land on the eye and don't melt. Beneath the cottonwoods, a hungry coyote has joined the eagle. I whisper an invitation to the scavengers. I thank the bison for providing them sustenance and then turn and snowshoe toward the road without a backward glance. I figure that I know what comes next.

As it turns out, I had no idea.

Though we moved the bison just hours ago, the news of the meal-waiting-to-happen went viral among the long-weekend visitors. By noon, the three pullouts and the road connecting them look like the scene of a nasty accident. A ranger SUV, lights flashing, sits before the first pullout. Another flashes after the last one. All three pullouts are jammed with vehicles surrounded by talkative visitors. Photographers perch atop a couple of vans. People mill around in the road. At one point, a gigantic tour bus rumbles up, stops in the middle of the road, but thankfully does not disgorge its contents.

On Saturday, the photographers get into a feeding frenzy when the Lamar Canyon wolf pack comes down from Druid Peak. Rangers stop traffic in both directions, giving ten wolves safe passage across the road. Still, with the machine gun-like clacking of motor-driven cameras and the wolves' aversion to humans, they take a long time to cross.

Once they reach the bison, one approaches the carcass, sniffs it and leaps back—I assume it's repulsed by the scent from our earlier handling. I feel guilty at my selfish need to touch the calf without considering the lingering human stench. A couple of other wolves are also repelled before the pack risks opening the carcass. Meanwhile, impatient ravens croak, the eagle observes from a cottonwood, and the coyote is nowhere to be seen.

On Monday afternoon, when most of the long-weekend visitors are home or driving there, Mary and I and just three others watch the well-fed Lamar Canyon pack cross the empty road only yards from us and trot along that ridge that leads up to Druid Peak. I feel blessed to be so close, but as I watch their nervous behavior, I also feel like a nuisance.

Three weeks and three snowstorms later, Mary and I return to the pullout where we loaded the yearling onto the sled. We are curious to see what remains of the carcass. The path we made for the bison's last ride has disappeared. We don our snowshoes and head across virgin snow toward the cottonwoods. We guess our way along but can't find the remains. We squat down in the snow and wait. Just as we are starting to feel too chilled to stay, a black-and-white flash zips by. The magpie lands about twenty yards away and starts walking and pecking.

We rise and move toward it, picking up a trail of magpie tracks, each a skinny Y. We spot strands of hair and fragments of bone and center ourselves in the debris field. Mary drops to all fours and starts sweeping away snow. A few inches below the surface, she uncovers a frozen rug of bison hide. Nearby, she discovers a blood-stained bottom jaw with unworn teeth. I dig around, come up with a hoof attached to a leg bone. I take off my glove and again feel the hoof's ridges.

When I look up from the hoof, something bright and blue and about ten yards away catches my eye. With respect I put the hoof down, snowshoe the distance, and tug a ragged piece of fabric from the snow. A piece of a hat? A towel? Hard to say from what remains, but it reeks with the pungent smell of wolf. I imagine the pups using the fabric as a pull toy while the adults—satiated after dining—doze.

I snowshoe back and kneel beside Mary. She turns to me and her eyes hold both sadness and curiosity. She nods toward where she has been digging, and we begin to cover the hide and put the bones back. The bison's return to earth isn't done yet, and we don't want to interfere.

In a month or two, when the snow thaws and spring greens this valley, hundreds of species of beetles and other insects will dine on these scraps. Anything left will begin breaking down into minerals that will enrich the soil and feed the grass. Where we now kneel in snow will be a sweet spot for bison grazing near the swollen Lamar River. A mother and her calf could be drawn here by the scent of new grass. The calf, still young enough to be mistaken for a big, red dog playing near the herd, will eat its fill, enriched by the yearling we pulled here.

Mary and I stand, hold hands, and snowshoe back toward the road, closing the circle on what began as a lark and became a touching farewell and funeral service.

Now, there's a bus to drive and cabins to clean.

8

From Asian Cattle to Yellowstone Bison

———

At first glance, Yellowstone's iconic bison—heads down and eating or heads up and staring—may look like cattle: slow moving, docile, dumb. But that's judging a bison by its cover and missing the magnificent story of an animal adapting to all that nature threw at it for millions of years. It's a story that begins and ends with cattle.

The ancestors of Yellowstone's bison were small cattle that lived in southern Asian two to three million years ago, according to Harold Picton in *Buffalo Natural History and Conservation.* Over the course of a million or so years, they grazed their way north, adapting to a colder, drier environment.

No one was around to record that long migration and slow adaptation. But I can imagine capturing it with time lapse photography taken over, say, 500,000 years. Playing that film back, we would watch that small Asian cow evolve. We would see its head grow larger and more massive, better suited for pushing away snow to uncover life-sustaining grasses. As the head grew heavier, a shoulder hump would appear, evidence of the muscle and bone required to lift and swing that bigger head. We would see the animal's hair grow longer for better protection against consistently colder temperatures.

And there would be adaptations that we couldn't see. Beneath the lengthening hair, the hide would grow thicker, providing more insulation against more cold. The animal would become better at producing and storing fat, the secret ingredient for surviving long winters devoid of nutritious grasses. Those changes and more would be passed on through hundreds of thousands of generations.

At the end of that time lapse photography, if we could position an original Asian cow next to the evolved animal, we would see differences so great that we'd need a name for the "new" animal. We could call it the Asian bison.

The Asian bison continued moving, migrated so far north that they reached the area now called Siberia and ran into the Bering Strait, a body of water too wet to graze and too wide to swim. Finally stopped in their tracks, they settled into northern living.

Then, around 200,000 years ago, the bison felt the icy touch of what would be the first of many climatic changes. Over tens of thousands of cold years, the ice in the Bering Strait and the bodies of water into which it flowed no longer melted after winter ended. Year-round sea ice formed, covering the oceans and lowering the sea level.

The Bering Strait is shallow in some places, and covers a wide ridge of land. As sea ice formed and sea level fell, that ridge seemed to rise ever so slowly until a bridge of solid land connected Siberia with what we now call Alaska. On that land bridge, grass seed, freed from icy water and exposed to a warm sun, sprouted and grew, creating an inviting pasture for the Asian bison. They followed their noses and grazed across the thousand-mile bridge to North America.

Eventually, temperatures rose, sea ice was no longer present year-round, and the sea level started to rise. Inch by inch—as the ice age warmed to a halt—the rising waters of the Bering Strait swallowed the land bridge. The bison that had grazed across from Asia could not return. But the bison did what they do best: graze, move, adapt. After tens of thousands of years of living on the North American continent, the Asian bison evolved into the North American bison.

The ups and downs of climate change continued, and as the average temperature dropped, snow that fell during one winter did not melt before the next winter arrived. For thousands of years snowfall accumulated, its sheer weight turning the snow below the surface into ice and creating glaciers. The glaciers became huge fences that corralled the bison in a pasture that stretched from South America, through North America, and even back across the re-exposed land bridge to Asia. The bison grazed the pasture, growing larger until the animal that began as a small Asian cow weighed as much as a Yellowstone bison weighs today. Even with American lions hunting and killing these large animals, their population swelled.

Later in this period of glaciation, the average temperature fell further, conditions grew harsher. The weak, the sick, and those that couldn't adapt died; the bison population fell. New glaciers formed, creating an impassable icy wall that cut the North American bison's pasture in two, locking some animals into Alaska and the Yukon, and the rest into what we now call the Great Plains.

Like a yo-yo, when the average temperature went down, it eventually came back up. And when it did, the ice melted and grasses sprouted. The bison ate and ate until the average plains bison weighed twice as much as the average bison in Yellowstone today. The animal had changed so much that it was now called the plains bison.

Around 7,000 years ago, the easy living ended and thousands of years of colder winters, hotter summers, and droughts in the Great Plains began. The plains bison rolled with nature's punches, adapting to survive. They slimmed down to today's smaller model and kept moving, increasing their population and grazing north into Canada, south into Mexico, west into the Rockies, and east into meadows along the Atlantic coast.

By the time European settlers arrived in the New World, 30-100 million bison roamed this continent. Early settlers were too busy conquering the wilderness to record a more accurate bison count for future historians. Whatever the starting number, historians agree that in less than three hundred years almost all the bison were gone. The bison's demise was not due to freezing winters and glaciation or scorching summers and drought. It wasn't due to disease or predators. No, by the 1840s—after millions of years of moving and adapting—the bison encountered something they couldn't walk away from or adapt to: the great migration of humans rumbling westward in wagon trains, searching for land and a brighter future.

Those emigrants making ruts across the Great Plains did not have refrigeration but did have to eat. And there, grazing within rifle range of their covered wagons, was a bounty of fresh meat. The feeding frenzy began. One group of emigrants in Kansas in the 1850s, for example, killed over 300 bison. Multiply that by the thousands of wagon trains crossing the plains and oh, how the mighty bison fell.

But hungry emigrants were just part of the bison's problem. Sports hunters with no intention of eating their prey killed thousands more. Fashion even played a part: the chilly Little Ice Age in the mid-1800s created a hot market for millions of warm buffalo hides. Then came the U.S. Calvary, killing bison as a way of eliminating the Plains Indians, whose culture depended on the bison; the Indians used the dung for fuel and almost every part of the animal for food, tools, clothing, and shelter.

But the straw that broke the bison's back was the transcontinental railroad. More specifically, the need to feed the thousands of workers laying the tracks. For about twenty years, commercial hunters supplied bison meat to the railroads. A good hunter could kill a hundred bison in one day and not even stampede the herd. Buffalo Bill Cody earned his name by supplying the railroads with 4,280 bison in less than eighteen months. (That would be the equivalent of one man with a rifle slaughtering all the bison that now roam Yellowstone.)

After fifty years of killing for food, sport, ethnic cleansing, or profit, almost no bison remained. Yellowstone contained the *only surviving wild herd*, and protecting even those few bison was a challenge for the U.S. Army, then responsible for the park. Poaching in Yellowstone was rampant and profitable: A bison head could fetch $300, the equivalent of about $7,000 today.

But while poachers were beheading bison, more and more park visitors were dazzled by Yellowstone's beauty and returning to their homes with stories of "Wonderland," as the park was then called. One of those visitors was a reporter for the popular magazine *Forest and Stream*. The reporter wrote about the 1894 capture of an infamous poacher and the laughingly light punishment he received. The poaching story touched a national nerve and led to an outcry for a law with teeth that would deter poaching. That quickly led to the passage of the Lacey Act, the first federal law protecting bison and other wildlife in Yellowstone.

Though now protected, the herd was ridiculously small. By 1900 only two dozen or so bison remained in Yellowstone. The government stepped in again, this time with money. Congress appropriated $15,000 for rebuilding Yellowstone's herd. That was not a lot of money, equivalent to only about $400,000 today. The project began by importing to Mammoth (the north entrance to the park) eighteen cows from northwest Montana and three bulls from Texas.

Within a few years, this so-called captive herd outgrew the Mammoth pens and was moved to the Lamar Valley. For about fifty years, bison were raised at the Lamar Buffalo

Ranch in the same way cattle are raised. There were fences south to the Lamar River, fences west to Slough Creek. To feed the herd, the valley floor was tilled and timothy and other kinds of non-native grasses were planted; they weren't called invasive species back then.

In the 1930s the captive herd was set free and started breeding with Yellowstone's few remaining wild bison. The free-roaming herd began to grow. And grow. And grow. Within twenty years, park officials feared that the large herd would overgraze the park. Bison were castrated, slaughtered, shipped out to zoos, and—ironically enough—donated to Native Americans. Finally, in 1968 park officials stopped managing the herd and let nature take its course.

Yellowstone turned out to be, as Robert Steelquist wrote in the *Greater Yellowstone Coalition Bison Field Guide,* a biological ark for bison. After one of the first and most successful restorations in the world, Yellowstone now has two herds totaling about 4,000 head. One roams the Lamar Valley. The other grazes in Hayden Valley or the Old Faithful area.

But this story does not have a happy ending.

Bison are safe within the park, but not welcome outside the park. Because some bison are infected with brucellosis, those that cross the boundary lines may be hazed back into the park, publicly hunted, or captured and shipped to slaughter. Brucellosis can be transferred to cattle, and ranchers and park officials fear this could happen if bison are allowed to roam outside the park. They believe this would endanger the health of the cattle and the profits of the ranchers. Sadly, the park's bison were originally infected with brucellosis by cattle that were raised within the park to feed Yellowstone's early visitors.

The bison's three-million-year-long journey from southern Asia, to Siberia, to Alaska, to the Yukon, and to the Great Plains has come to an abrupt and unnatural end. These animals began their journey as small cattle. And have stopped their journey because of cattle. Yellowstone is now a large holding pen in which these once free-roaming creatures are controlled by humans, the same species that drove them to the brink of extinction.

9

A Conspiracy of Ravens

———

As I walk away from the ranch and down the middle of the snow-covered main road, a raven passes just above me. I hear the creaking made by its powerful wings with their four-foot span. I step to the side of the road, stop, and watch the raven go. I'm in no rush today.

Before leaving the ranch, I checked our schedule of upcoming seminars. We have three busy "Wolf Weeks" ahead, each a five-day seminar filled with excited wolf watchers and some sixteen-hour work days. Before the crush hits, I am heading for the slow quiet of my spot in the cottonwoods to lounge, look, and listen. I have a pair of binoculars in a daypack and a spotting scope mounted on a tripod slung over my shoulder. The temperature is pleasant, hovering above freezing. Today's off and on snow is currently off.

I watch the departing raven grow smaller and smaller until it is just a black squiggle against the distant, white Absaroka Mountains. Even after the bird disappears, I stay still, enjoying the simplicity of watching nothing in particular and listening to resounding silence.

During the seminars I have supported so far, we have seen hundreds of ravens. And most of the time ignored them, except as tools for finding wolves. Yellowstone's wolves are one of the world's so-called "charismatic megafauna," the movie stars of the animal kingdom, employed by activists to further ecological causes. Ravens, on the other hand, are the opposite of charismatic megafauna. I guess we could call them mundane minifauna, simply a part of the landscape, like their crow cousins in a city park, or seagulls at the beach.

But after months of watching ravens thrive in a harsh and frigid environment by befriending wolves and then stealing food from them, I wondered if ravens weren't more than what biologists call a kleptoparasite. So I dug into the row of bird books in the bunkhouse library, and often found myself surprised—even amazed—by the raven. The more I learned, the more I came to believe that we don't give this bird the respect it deserves.

The raven may be the most successful of all Yellowstone's birds. So says Terry McEneaney, and he should know; he was the Yellowstone staff ornithologist and is the author of *Birds of Yellowstone*. He writes, "Its success lies in its ability to adapt to humans, to live in a hostile environment, to eat a wide variety of food items, and to live in a wide variety of habitats."

Wide variety of habitats is almost an understatement. Ravens live across the entire northern hemisphere (as do their wolf benefactors), from the frozen arctic to scorching deserts. They have even been seen flying at over 20,000 feet on the snowy slopes of Mt. Everest.

Standing on the Yellowstone roadside, I hear the growl of an approaching pickup truck. I turn away from the road, and hike down the small embankment toward Rose Creek and the stand of cottonwoods I have claimed as my little territory.

Reaching the stand of six tall and wide-spaced trees, I stop, close my eyes, and take a deep breath of crisp air. As I purse my lips and exhale, I sound like a tire with a slow leak. I open my eyes and lean the scope and tripod against the trunk of a cottonwood. I take off my pack, dig out the binoculars, and drape their strap around my neck. Then I drop the pack onto the snow, bring the binoculars to my eyes, and start scanning the valley floor for wildlife. I turn a very slow circle, stopping every time I see an animal-like shape. But they are all imposters: log dogs, boulder bison, and rock ravens. No matter; this slow perusal allows me to feel a part of this place, in it instead of passing through it.

Just before I complete the circle, I spot a *real* raven sitting in the branches of a downed tree out near the frozen Lamar River. This could be good: Where there are ravens there may be a carcass or canid. Then I chuckle and chide myself; there I go using the raven as little more than a meat-activated wolf detector.

As I start glassing the raven, a black-and-white flash at the edge of the binoculars' circular field of vision catches my eye. I swing the binoculars toward it and focus on a magpie flying up the valley, toward the raven. A smaller cousin of the raven, a magpie is almost all black, with a belly and wing tips as white as the clouds high above. The bird darts between the snowflakes that have just resumed falling. Behind the bird rises the white slope of Specimen Ridge, painted with dark swaths of shadowy conifers. The scene in the binoculars is like a black-and-white movie, and the gurgling of Rose Creek provides the perfect soundtrack.

The raven watches the magpie as it descends in dips, flies past, and lands nearby. The raven turns its head and its beak opens and a croak emerges. Is it talking to the magpie?

That's possible. While Poe's famous raven may have been limited to "Nevermore," scientists have found wild ravens to be much more talkative. They have shouts of alarm, cries for claiming territory, calls that comfort, and even tones made when in flight. An instructor told me that ravens have a call that they make only when wolves are nearby. And ravens can mimic other sounds including those of a missing mate or human speech. So maybe Poe's raven did actually say that famous word. (But who was it mimicking?)

Their communication skills probably help these birds work together, something else they do well. Flock members share sentry duty and childcare. They show—or tell—other ravens where food can be found and help each other gather food. They mob intruders and use stones to bomb predators that approach their nests. Talking to one another and working together must be signs of intelligence. And, in fact, the raven has one of the biggest brains in the bird world.

But right now, that solo raven on the downed log is not demonstrating much of an IQ. It's just sitting and gazing—quite like I am. Maybe that log is *its* favorite place and it's watching me and wondering what I'm going to do next. I move the binoculars from the raven and begin another visual lap of the valley. I see no other animals, hear nothing except snow hitting my jacket. The silence pleases me.

Completing the circle, I return my gaze to the fallen log. Now there are two ravens, sitting side-by-side and facing in my direction. I laugh aloud as I wonder: If I keep circling will the pair increase to a flock—or a so-called "conspiracy" or "unkindness" of ravens? Those labels smack of disrespect. Especially when compared to the names for flocks of other common birds: a *parliament* of owls, *bouquet* of pheasants, *charm* of finches.

The two ravens on the log start to preen one another, and I smile and exclaim, "Oh, maybe they're a mating pair." If so, they are right on Frank Craighead's schedule, found in his book, *For Everything There Is a Season.* For more than forty years, Craighead has recorded the comings and goings of birds and other animals around his home just south of Yellowstone. He says that in March ravens will choose their mates, defend a nesting territory, preen, and even play.

An instructor once described to me how a raven played with just-emerged pups at a wolf den. He watched the bird sneak up behind a pup, grab the pup's tail with its beak, pull, and then let the startled youngster go. The pup in turn chased the raven that hopped away. The two repeated this game of pull and chase, with no harm to either player.

I wonder if early bonding like this makes the raven one of the pack in the developing mind of a young wolf. Do pups see ravens as funny-shaped pack mates? Is that why grown wolves chase ravens from a carcass but rarely kill them?

This is so different from how a wolf treats a coyote, another kleptoparasite. Wolves will kill a thieving coyote. Yet a conspiracy of ravens can conspire to steal way more than a coyote. A single raven can eat and cache about two pounds of meat. One time I counted thirty ravens on a kill. That's sixty pounds of meat flying away. With no ravens injured. Convincing evidence that ravens and wolves share a special bond.

Ravens had a similar bond with coyotes when they were the top dogs in Yellowstone. Adolph Murie, that researcher who studied coyotes in the 1930s when there were no wolves in the park, also observed ravens. It was, I guess, impossible not to observe these ubiquitous birds. In *Ecology of the Coyote in Yellowstone*, Murie wrote, "They are interested in each other's actions; the raven watches the coyote and the coyote watches the raven. If one has found a source of food, he is sure to be joined by the other sooner or later." He observed ravens playing with coyotes as well as warning them of approaching intruders.

Right now, the two ravens in my binoculars have no intruders to worry about, and they are content to preen one another. I want to take a closer look and see if one is larger and therefore a male. I put away the binoculars, grab the spotting scope, extend its legs, and set them onto the snow. Two of the three legs bust through the snow's crust with a loud crunch, sinking six inches. I make some height adjustments and then zoom the scope on the ravens. I swivel the scope from one bird to the other, sizing each up.

The bird on the left is much larger. So maybe this is a mating pair and he is the male. I lock the scope in place with the male centered in the glass. When he turns his head to face the female, his beak is in profile, and I am struck by how large it is compared to his head. A raven has one of the largest beaks of all perching birds.

But in beaks, size isn't everything. Shape's the thing. A raptor, such as an eagle, has a hooked and curved beak that operates as a killing and opening tool. The raven's beak, though large, has only a slight curve and is not that effective at ripping and tearing. That's why ravens depend on wolves and coyotes to open the food bank.

Ravens can use their beaks to kill smaller prey such as rodents or young rabbits. That must be gruesome if it happens as described in *Bird Tracks and Signs*: Ravens bludgeon their prey to death with repeated pecks to the skull. Even after killing the animal, ravens may have trouble opening the carcass. So they will peck at the prey's eyes. Once through the eye, they peck toward the brain. (Now, that's an *unkindness* of ravens.)

Ravenous ravens are omnivores and not particular about what they eat. They will gobble up maggots and beetles on a kill long after the bones have been picked clean. They will nibble bone marrow if the bones were cracked by others or if the bones are small enough for them to open. Bones are not all that ravens can open; these intelligent birds have learned to unzip zippers and unsnap snaps. The National Park Service warns Yellowstone visitors that an unattended pack is raven bait.

In my scope, the male raven bounces up and down, fluffs the rough feathers around his neck and twitches his wings, preparing to fly. Perhaps I'll be lucky and see these two soar into the synchronized flight of breeding pairs. Or maybe—as ravens have been known to do—they will play with one another while flying, one dropping a twig, the other swooping in to catch it before it hits the ground.

The male croaks once and takes off down the valley. The female watches, calls, and pursues. They fly straight and fast with no acrobatics, no twig swapping. As I swivel the scope to keep them in sight, I wish them a long and productive life together.

Ravens can live up to twenty-one years in the wild and they mate for life. This pair could have four to six little ravens leaving the nest by late June or mid-July. And that's good because the world needs more birds like these: curious and intelligent, social and adaptable, resourceful and problem solvers. Come to think of it, the world could use more people like that, too.

The sun is disappearing and dinner is calling this aging omnivore back to the ranch. I put on my pack and take one more look around the valley, savoring today's quiet raven watching from the cottonwoods. As I sling the scope over my shoulder and turn toward the road, I find myself ruminating on how ravens were once viewed as vermin and killed without mercy. But they not only survived, they thrived. Ravens have learned to live with humans and that's no easy task. The raven deserves our respect, even if it's mini instead of mega and mundane instead of charismatic.

10

Bus Driver in the Temple of Wolves

It's ten below zero, not yet dawn, and time to prepare for today's sunrise service. To the west, Specimen Ridge cradles the March full moon. I walk to my fourteen-passenger bus where ice glistens on the windshield and windows. Attacking the crust with a long-handled scraper wrecks the dark silence with squeals and squeaks, cracks and pops. When I stop to catch my breath, a coyote sings his thanks from nearby Ranger Hill. He would probably like me to kill the engine and cut the fumes. But I can't; I must warm the bus for my soon-to-arrive passengers.

A while later, fed and caffeinated, the seminar participants bounce to the bus, cheeks burning crimson in the cold. Low morning sun lights their faces; first-day excitement widens their eyes. Nylon snow pants swish with each step, and snow crunches beneath heavy, insulated boots.

Once they fill the bus, I climb aboard and bid them a hearty, "Good morning!" I count heads covered with hoods and wool caps, some sporting the logo of the Lamar Buffalo

Ranch. They are here for the first "Wolf Week" of the winter, a five-day field seminar, watching, hearing, studying—and some would say worshipping—wolves, in one of nature's best wintry temples.

I settle into the driver's seat and point the bus down the snow-covered driveway. When I reach its junction with the main road, I will drive where today's instructor, Brad, directs. It's his job to bring the worshippers close to what one park ranger calls Yellowstone's "spiritual dogs." Their abundance makes the Lamar Valley the world's best place to observe free-ranging wolves. The goal of a Wolf Week is to do just that.

Brad tells me to turn west and head for Dorothy's pullout. The few roadside pullouts that are plowed during winter have names given by wolf watchers, names from the mundane to the picturesque: from Straightaway to Hitching Post, from Midway to Wrecker, from Trashcan to Hellroaring. At Dorothy's—named after a researcher—I pull the bus out and cut the engine. I am instantly buried beneath an avalanche of noise as my eager passengers gather cameras, binoculars, thermoses, and backpacks and clunk, clunk, clunk down the bus steps. The racket fades as they shuffle away to the far edge of the pullout and gather. Spotting scope tripods clank and ping as they are set up. The congregants are ready for the service.

Brad uses his right hand—it's clad in a camouflage-patterned glove—to adjust his scope. A few moments later, he says in a hushed tone, "Over there, on that skyline ridge. By that big fir at the edge of the sunny snowfield. That's the Lamar Canyon pack." Eye to the scope, he provides a running commentary about the pack's black alpha male, his larger brother, and the gray alpha female.

"Oh, I see them!" a tall woman hunched over her scope exclaims.

"Where? Where?" pleads a white-bearded man, head swiveling, hand above his eyes to shade the sun.

I ask if I can adjust his scope, and he nods, excited. I scan left and then up and then right until the alpha female stands centered in the glass. I trade places with him as she looks toward the pullout and raises her head skyward. Her neck stretches and her mouth opens. Two seconds later—she's about a half mile away—her howl arrives, almost lost amid the roadside chatter and clatter as other visitors arrive and vie for space in the small pullout.

"Howling! Listen! They're howling!" a woman yells, hand cupped around her ear.

"Quiet! Everybody quiet!" Brad, the high priest, commands, hands in the air. His blue eyes are as intense as those of a hunting hawk.

One by one the congregants grow still. Not a word, a swish, a cough.

Another howl arrives, high and wavering. The alpha male joins in, his addition low and solid. A clumsy black pup with long legs and big paws adds his tenor line to the choir.

A woman beside me whispers, "Beautiful. Just beautiful."

I smile at her and nod. I've seen people cry at the sight or sound of their first Yellowstone wolf.

More howls bounce off Specimen Ridge, haunting harmonies in this ancient, high-ceilinged cathedral.

Brad cocks his head and whispers, "Listen for an answer."

The teenage girl who's been busy adjusting her hat, playing with her hair, straightening her coat, even she stops and listens with intent. She moves over and snuggles against her mom, who hugs her and offers a view through the scope.

"Wow. Oh, wow," the girl breathes.

Another convert.

From the east, in the sun's warming rays drifts an answering howl. Another pack? A turf battle? Other Lamar Canyon pack members returning the morning greeting? Only the wolves know. We can just listen and wonder and feel our spirits soar as we eavesdrop on these giant dogs speaking to each other in their wild language.

I tiptoe toward a man with a camera pressed to his face. He squints into a huge telephoto lens, checks this and adjusts that. The motor drive clicks away the silence, like an old manual typewriter banging out a headline. He lifts his finger, kills the motor. He checks the images, frowns, and tweaks the technology.

Meanwhile, in front of him, steam rises off the road and disappears into a sky too blue. The morning light glints off the camera and heightens the red of his jacket, the black of his pants, the green of his boots. I'm struck again by how the presence of wolves intensifies everything.

The howling stops and the pack beds down. Minutes pass and one by one people stir. Fabric whispers and conversations revive. A car door slams. An engine fires and tires crunch over snow. The sunrise service is over; the congregants are leaving.

Brad turns to the group, grins, and asks, "Nice way to start the day?"

"Awesome!"

"I want more."

"What's next?"

"Let's head east," Brad says, pointing toward the distant Absaroka Mountains. "We might find those wolves that answered."

The congregants pack up the scopes, which I load into the rear of the bus. I walk the pullout in a final gear check and find an orphan glove in the snow. I climb into the bus, pull the doors shut, and count heads. A bright-eyed man in the backseat shoots me an exaggerated wink, followed by a high thumbs-up. I laugh and return the gesture. I hold up the glove, and a heavyset man, already becoming known for leaving a trail of gear, raises his hand shyly. I slip him the glove.

Seat belts click as I turn and slide behind the steering wheel. I drive toward the morning sun, searching for the next pullout in this temple, the next part of today's wolf worship.

11

The Archbishop and the Wolf Wars

Two days later, I'm with the same group of participants, and at sunrise—before we even board the bus—nine of the wolves from the Mollie's pack walk east up the Lamar Valley right in front of the ranch, while ten of the Lamar Canyon pack head west up Ranger Hill. Two wolf packs—well aware of each other—and we are smack in the middle. No spotting scopes needed. What a gift!

After the wolves go their separate ways, we board the bus and go ours. The morning's gifts continue; we spot big horn sheep, bison, ravens, magpies, a bald eagle, and an otter that is busy slipping in and out of a hole in the frozen Lamar River.

Now, I am driving us to what may be the high point of our day even after such a glorious morning. We are going to a roadside rendezvous with Rick McIntyre, who has agreed to give one of his much sought-after talks.

If instructors like Brad are priests in this temple, McIntyre is the Archbishop. He has earned this title while choosing to stay for many years—he is approaching Medicare age—in a low-level job as a biological technician for the Wolf Project. He has the knowledge and experience to be much higher up. He just loves watching wolves.

I mean he *loves* watching wolves; the Archbishop is downright religious about it. Two years ago *Outside Magazine* featured him in a profile piece. The reporter used statistics to capture the depth of what he called McIntyre's obsession with wolf watching. During one ten-year period, he worked every day, seven days a week for at least 3,500 consecutive days. (That's with no rest on the Sabbath, I might add.). He told the reporter that he did catch a cold back in 1997, but that did not keep him home. And this in a job that requires climbing out of bed well before 4 a.m. on summer days and by 5 a.m. on cold winter days.

Regardless of the season, his time in the temple stretches from sunrise to sunset, though he often allows himself a nap in the middle of the day—just like the wolves. After so many years of being seen as he peers into a spotting scope in a pullout or scans with binoculars from roadside ridges, he is as well known to wolf watchers as Old Faithful is to geyser gazers.

Ahead, I spot McIntyre's SUV with its rooftop thicket of radio antennas. It's parked in a crowded pullout, which is no surprise; his SUV draws visitors like a wolf kill draws ravens. (Visitors hungry for wolves are actually *told* to look for a lemon-yellow SUV.) And there's McIntyre, standing a bit taller than most everyone, wearing NPS green, and cradling the handheld H-shaped antenna that receives signals from radio-collared wolves.

I'm lucky to find a space big enough to park the bus. After my passengers scoot down the front steps, they form a large horseshoe in front of McIntyre. I close up the bus and slip into a spot within the group, one row back from him. He puts away the antenna and instructs us to come closer so that his speech won't disturb the pullout's other wolf watchers. After we squeeze in, he asks in his quiet voice if we saw the Mollie's pack this morning. Our reply is a wave of excited nods and murmurs.

McIntyre shakes his head and grins. Though he speaks with groups almost every day, often in a pullout like today with the temperature below freezing, or sometimes in the classroom at the ranch after a long day in the field, he never appears to tire of sharing his knowledge and his audience's excitement.

His attention is drawn from us to the squawking of one of the two radios protruding from the many pockets on his well-worn vest. This is what wolf watchers call the "Rick Radio," the one paid and volunteer helpers use all day to feed him information on wolf activity and whereabouts. He listens, whispers a short reply that I can't make out, grabs a digital voice recorder from another vest pocket, and dictates a note. From field observations like this, he has produced, according to that *Outside Magazine* reporter, more than 8,000 pages of transcribed notes, many filed in three-ring binders. McIntyre's boss told the reporter that McIntyre was proud that his volumes of notes now contained more words than the Bible. (A Google search surprised me with just how many words that is. The King James Bible contains 788,280 in 1,189 chapters.)

McIntyre stows the voice recorder, focuses again on our group, smiles, and says nothing. Maybe he is thinking of what to say next. We wait in silence for the Archbishop to begin his homily. Finally, he launches into a chapter of local wolf war history, a topic that always intrigues, and one he has observed firsthand. In the time I've worked here, I've listened to many people recite wolf history—it could as well be described as a wolf soap opera. No one is better than McIntyre at keeping the story straight and compelling. I inch closer to the man in front of me so that I won't miss a word.

"There were three packs of wolves," he begins, "captured in Alberta in 1995 and brought to Yellowstone." He describes how they were held in pens so that they would acclimate to the park. One pack of six wolves, the Crystal Creek pack, was set free in March 1995. They took over the Lamar Valley, a year-round home to elk, the preferred meal of these wolves.

In January 1996, the reintroduction continued with four more packs imported from Canada. One was acclimated in the Rose Creek pen that is just a mile from the Lamar Buffalo Ranch, in the shadow of Druid Peak, for which the pack was named. (A druid was a pre-Christian priest. The peak was given that name in 1885. It seems that Yellowstone has evoked religious references for many years.) In April 1996, the Druid Peak pack was released.

"And we assumed," McIntyre says, "that since almost all of Yellowstone was unoccupied, they had their choice of living almost anywhere." He pauses for a moment and scans the Lamar Valley, maybe to make sure he is not missing a wolf sighting. "However, they surprised us by deciding that they wanted this territory, even though it was already taken."

The Druids would not get the valley without a fight. Wolves are fiercely territorial, marking boundaries with sprays of urine. Intruders ignoring these olfactory borders are almost guaranteed a battle. McIntyre says that must have been what the Druids wanted. They tracked down and attacked the Crystal Creek wolves, killing that pack's alpha male. The surviving Crystal Creek wolves retreated about twenty miles south to Pelican Valley, where they discovered that deep winter snow drives out the elk. This leaves only bison as winter prey, animals that are bigger and tougher, more aggressive and dangerous than elk.

A wolf pack will sift and sort an elk herd and select one animal to attack. The rest of the elk will avoid that fight. Not so with bison. A bison herd will encircle a weak member to protect it from attack. Even if wolves manage to separate one bison from the herd, other members may charge the pack. Bison have been known to surround one of the herd that has died from natural causes to protect the body from scavengers—though the herd did not do this for the dying calf which I watched coyotes kill and consume a month ago.

But the Crystal Creek wolves grew bigger and tougher, evolved into bison hunters, and made Pelican Valley their year-round home. In time, the pack was renamed the Mollie's pack in memory of Mollie Beattie, the first female director of the U.S. Fish and Wildlife Service and instrumental in the return of wolves to Yellowstone. Due to failing health, she had to resign her job after three productive years. She died from brain cancer at age forty-nine.

Having a Yellowstone wolf pack take your name is quite an honor. Only two other packs carry a person's name. One is the Leopold pack, named after the ecologist Aldo Leopold. The other is the Chief Joseph pack, named after the great leader of the Nez Perce tribe. All other packs are named after the geographic area in which they form.

Back in the pullout, McIntyre reads our faces as he reveals that he has often wondered if the Mollie's would one day try to reclaim their ancestral home in the Lamar Valley. Over the ensuing years the Mollie's did periodically swagger back to the valley to hunt elk and fight with resident wolves. Wolves almost always attack an opposing pack's alphas, and during one battle the Mollie's killed the Druid Peak alpha female. The body count, the Archbishop says, was now even: one alpha killed in each pack.

Years and generations of wolves came and went as McIntyre watched pups in both packs grow to adulthood and have pups of their own. In the fall of 2009, he heard that the Mollie's and Druids had clashed up the Lamar River.

"In that battle, once again, an alpha wolf was killed," McIntyre tells us, "the alpha female of the Druid Peak pack. So now the Mollie's were ahead in this war of attrition."

The death of the Druid alpha female left the alpha male with no one to mate with. All the pack's females were his daughters, and wolves have a strong instinct to not breed with close relatives. Though he was the alpha male of a powerful and large pack—at one time it had thirty-seven members—

he surprised everyone by leaving the Druids in search of a new mate.

"He essentially resigned his position in an attempt to start over again," McIntyre says in his characteristic way of describing wolves in fitting human terms. His face grows sad when he adds that the old alpha did not survive the dangerous search.

With both alphas gone, the Druid Peak pack faded away. While that ended the generational battle between the Druids and Mollie's, wolf wars never end. One scientist calls territorial battles a form of wolf population control, and wolves killing wolves is the leading natural cause of wolf death. (Though I fear that the leading cause of death may change now that wolves are off the federal endangered species list in some western states and in the gun sights of hunters.)

With the Druids out of the picture and the Mollie's back in Pelican Valley eating bison, the Lamar Valley was claimed by the up and coming Lamar Canyon pack, another group that McIntyre had watched evolve.

"Just around the time that the Druid pack fell apart," McIntyre says, "a great female showed up on the scene." She became the alpha female of the Lamar Canyon pack and was known to wolf watchers as 06 (pronounced "oh six") because she was born in 2006. She had led an independent life and had casual relationships with a number of males, breeding with at least five. But she left each one and returned to her independent ways. "She seemed to be searching for the right situation and didn't find it."

But in early 2010 she met two brothers, both black, half her age and inexperienced. "I guess that's what she was looking for," he says, laughing. Chuckles ripple through our enthralled group. "She's been with them ever since. She's definitely the brains of the operation." He pauses as if he's delivered the next line before and wants to savor it. "The two males are just smart enough to know that their lives are going to be great as long as they do everything they're told."

"Like me," yells a husband, off to my right. We all crack up and his wife punches him in the side.

McIntyre laughs at their antics and begins to speak, but howling from across the road stops him. He cocks his head, listens, and tells us that we are probably hearing 06 and the two brothers. I shake my head in admiration that he knows Yellowstone's wolves as individuals—there are, after all, a hundred living in the park right now.

An answering howl comes from farther away, and he says with a grin, "Let's listen for a second."

While we marvel in silence at the howling, he whispers a dictation on the time, location, and duration—more chapter and verse for the Archbishop's Bible-sized binders. When the howling stops, he tells us that the Lamars have been in this call-and-response with other wolves since this morning.

"Do the Lamars know who they're howling at?" asks a young woman from the back row.

"That's an excellent question," he says, a sincere statement he makes often. "We think that if wolves are only a few miles apart, by the sound of the howling they can identify individuals."

As he just identified 06.

McIntyre falls silent, perhaps waiting for another howl. When our group starts to stir, he continues the wolf war saga, in which the Mollie's are now fighting the Lamars. He tells us that the Mollie's recently made the twenty-mile trek from Pelican Valley back to the Lamar Valley. Upon arrival, they skirmished with two other packs, killing several members of one and the alpha male of another. Then they heard the Lamars howling. The Lamars didn't know it, but the Mollie's were right up the hill. After the howl, the Mollie's did something unusual: They did not howl back. Instead of a call-and-response, the Mollie's raised their tails and charged downhill in a surprise attack. The Lamars saw them and the two packs converged.

"At the last moment 06 made the correct decision," McIntyre says. "It would be safer for her family not to fight that battle at that time. Unfortunately, the Mollie's wolves had caught one of her black pups and were beating it up." A Lamar adult ran close to the pup and distracted the Mollie's, who then chased the adult. The pup just lay there, looking dead. "A few minutes later, the pup miraculously jumped up and ran off, later united with the pack, and is now doing fine."

Our collective sigh of relief creates a little cloud of vapor that drifts into the clear blue sky. Two men to my left exchange a knuckle tap.

McIntyre tells us that two months have passed since that skirmish. Now it's breeding season, and the Mollie's—as we witnessed at sunrise—are back. He says this puts 06 in a tough spot. "She's under a lot of stress from the attack. She's pregnant and thinking about denning and having new pups."

McIntyre believes that this morning, when the Mollie's passed the Lamars near the ranch, the Mollie's *chose* not to attack. "They had a nonaggression understanding today," he says, "and we don't know if that will change or not. The packs were somewhat evenly matched, and if two groups of wolves feel they're equal in numbers then they may not fight. But if one side greatly outnumbers the other, they will probably try to attack. So we're in the middle of this thing that's been going on for about sixteen years, and who knows how it's going to end up."

Though the Mollie's seem like an invincible pack that could reclaim the Lamar Valley, we learn from McIntyre that they are not indestructible. Last year, the longtime alpha pair of the Mollie's died. The pack has no alpha male but does have a new alpha female. All the other pack members may be too closely related to breed with her. Several other females are also ready to breed, and they may have to split from the pack to find males to which they are not related.

McIntyre translates wolf dilemmas such as these into human terms. "Like people, wolves are constantly dealing with new, complicated situations, and they have to make decisions about what to do. Since they have different personalities, we never know for sure what they'll end up doing."

This saga segues into a sermon as the Archbishop ratchets up the comparison. "If you compare wolves with bees or ants, the differences are striking. Social insects are essentially born programmed into a certain role. You could say they have no choice, no free will. But, like us, wolves have plenty of free will. They can do whatever they want."

"Is there a risk," the man in front of me asks, "in your putting human values on these animals?"

McIntyre pauses, looks down at the snow. I'll bet he has been challenged on this many times before, perhaps most often by fact-minded scientists who want his data but not his opinions. When he looks up, he smiles, and says, "A lot of times people will say don't be *anthropomorphic,* which essentially means assuming that animals have the same emotions and motivations as people do. But what usually isn't said is that there's an opposite danger. That's being *anthropocentric* and making the mistake of assuming that our species is the *only one* that has emotions, feelings, and free will."

With that thought, the Archbishop wraps up the sermon. His day is far from ending, with more observations to make, more notes to take. (His word count must be sneaking up on a million.) He answers a few questions and then says he has to drive to another wolf sighting. He doesn't say where.

I'm not surprised that he is closed mouthed about the location. If he told us or the wolf watchers around us where he was going, this pullout would empty, and he would be driving at the head of a long parade. Instead, he leaves with no fanfare.

As the lemon-yellow SUV disappears around a bend, we climb aboard our bus. Driving back toward the ranch, I catch snippets of my passengers reliving the wolf wars and sharing their excitement at meeting *the* Rick McIntyre. Even though I've heard the Archbishop many times before, I feel the same way.

12

It Takes a Village to Protect a Pack

John stops his truck where the ranch driveway meets the main road, looks both ways, and wonders aloud, "Hmm, left or right? East or west?" He scratches his neatly trimmed auburn beard. His thin mustache is almost blond, and he reminds me of a young Patrick Swayze. When he turns left and accelerates, light snowfall dances in the beams of the truck's headlights. A moment later we spot the lemon-yellow SUV going in the opposite direction.

John snatches his handheld Rick Radio from the console and blurts, "Unit One, this is Unit Six. We're wondering if you're getting any signals this morning."

From John's radio comes McIntyre's short, soft reply, "Let's talk in person. One Clear."

Two days have passed since the Archbishop's roadside sermon on wolf wars, and the group that heard him preach ended their Wolf Week yesterday. Amidst handshakes and hugs and promises to stay in touch, they left the temple with several converts among them. A new group of seminar participants checked in to the ranch a few hours later, and their Wolf Week starts today. This morning their fresh excitement fills the bunkhouse dining room along with the aroma of pancakes and coffee. In an hour or so, I will be driving them and John, their instructor, to their first sunrise service.

But now, John and I are slipping away in his pickup truck for some private wolf watching before the sun climbs over Druid Peak. In pursuit of McIntyre, John makes a three-point turn and we catch up with him two pullouts down the road, where he's parked next to Doug, one of his volunteer wolf watchers. McIntyre tells John that he has not yet received signals from any radio-collared wolves.

About a third of all Yellowstone wolves wear a collar that carries a box that transmits GPS data or radio signals. McIntyre searches for those radio signals with his H-shaped antenna and special receiver. Finding a wolf's signals is like listening to the radio while traveling through the night on the interstate: Stations come and go as you drive into and out of their range. Each collared wolf is a four-legged radio station. Instead of broadcasting talk or tunes, each collar broadcasts a unique combination of clicks and beeps. That is what McIntyre listens for as he leaves the pullout and drives west.

We follow, our heads swiveling, hoping for a glimpse of wolves. As John drives, I ask how he landed his job in Yellowstone. He tells me that a couple of years ago he graduated from college with a degree in poultry science. This qualified him, he jokes, to be a chicken farmer. He tried it, worked for a corporate poultry producer, but found the job unfulfilling. He quit to travel in Europe and there stumbled into his first guiding gig. He kept freelance guiding until he ran out of money and returned home to Texas. Wondering what to do next, he heard about a guide training course offered through the Yellowstone Association. He scraped together the tuition, attended, and was offered a job as an instructor with the Association.

He's been working in Yellowstone for a year, a short stint for an instructor. At twenty-nine years old, he's climbing a steep learning curve in a park the size of Delaware and Rhode Island combined that showcases one of the most diverse populations of free-roaming large animals on earth. To speed his progress, he starts almost every day scouting on his own time for wildlife and more knowledge. I'm excited about this chance to learn with—and from—John this morning and to get to know him better.

Ahead of us, McIntyre's SUV stops in the middle of the road, emergency flashers blinking. John pulls up right behind him.

The Rick Radio squawks, "Unit Six, this is One. Can you back up?"

"Oops." John laughs and puts the truck in reverse. As it inches backwards, he says to me, "Look up there in front of Rick's SUV."

Through the snow-misted windshield, just beyond the lemon-yellow SUV that is also backing up, dark shapes of wolves crowd the roadside in the faint pre-dawn light.

"Whoa, that's close," I whisper, more from wonder than any worry that I'll spook the animals.

"Can you get a count?" John asks as he stops the truck.

I scan and count. "Ten. This must be the Lamar Canyon pack."

From the Rick Radio comes, "Unit Fifty, this is Unit One." McIntyre is calling Doug. "What's your location?"

Doug's cryptic reply: "Coyote."

Translation: Doug is at the pullout the wolf watchers call Coyote.

He's vague because so many visitors have purchased radios, found the Rick Radio frequency, and monitor it from sunup to sundown. As soon as they hear the location of a wolf sighting, they start driving, looking for McIntyre's SUV. This deluge of cars can flood a pullout, create traffic problems, and scare away the very animals that the visitors rushed to see.

Ahead of us, McIntyre has parked in the middle of the road. He steps out and dons his Day-Glo orange vest with Wolf Project written in big black letters across the back. The Wolf Project has studied the wolves since reintroducing them to Yellowstone. They do this with few employees and many volunteers. Most of the volunteers are young college graduates looking for experience and a stepping stone to a coveted—and highly competitive—job as a wildlife biologist in a national park. There's also a network of retirees, like Doug, willing to stand for hours in sub-zero temperatures several days a week—or more—to feed McIntyre info.

McIntyre reaches through the driver's side window of his SUV and brings out his handheld radio. His breath billows as he says, "Unit Fifty, have any cars passed you in the last few minutes going west?"

"No cars," Doug replies.

"Would you let me know if they do?" McIntyre requests as he climbs back into his SUV.

In addition to studying wolves, McIntyre has to worry about their interactions with humans, especially when the wolves are near this plowed public road, the lifeline of visitor activity. One possible problem interaction would be a wolf attacking a human, but that's unlikely; there has never been an attack in Yellowstone. The more pressing problem arises when familiarity breeds habituation. Park officials have had to kill two wolves that lost their native fear of humans. This road is one place habituation happens, as wolf watchers use it in ever-increasing numbers. During a recent winter 50,000 visitors entered the park on this road.

Right now, however, traffic is light, with just McIntyre's SUV, John's truck, Doug's SUV, and one visitor's car. But once word gets out that the wolves are close to the road—and it will get out—this road and all nearby pullouts will fill quickly and take on the air of a small carnival in a church parking lot.

That human desire to watch wolves could be a trait that helped our species survive. Mark Derr, an author and expert on wolves and dogs, believes that tens of thousands of years ago early humans watched hunting wolves stampede herds and then carefully select their prey. The humans, who had been hunting adult prey of both sexes, learned from the wolves to take only females too old to reproduce, or young males. This left in the herd females who could reproduce and males of breeding age. Their offspring would replenish the herd and the food supply of humans and wolves.

The possibility of humans learning from wolves leads me back to thinking about McIntyre's roadside sermon and how he has been criticized for giving wolves human traits. Now I wonder if there is also a converse of that: We must learn to see ourselves in terms of wolf traits. If we understood how we are more like than unlike the wolf, would we fear, hate, and kill it? Maybe we would. Just as wolves kill, but don't eat, coyotes. Maybe we kill wolves because we are driven on some deep level—just as wolves are driven—to cut the competition.

As John and I sit parked in the middle of the road, his truck flashers clicking, he stares through the windshield at the wolves. He's a keen observer with the eyesight of a hawk, like all the instructors with whom I've worked.

"I'm wondering," he says, "if there're one or two wolves over on the other side of the road because of how the ones in the road are staring in that direction."

The radio interrupts his wondering. "OK, John, let's go forward. And Doug, tell me what you can see ahead of me."

McIntyre has just recruited John and his truck to help orchestrate all movement near the wolves. I'm glad to be tagging along, watching what happens behind the scenes, and learning how it takes a village to protect a pack.

We drive forward, following the yellow SUV's flashers, and turn off the road into Dorothy's pullout. The sun is not yet above Druid Peak, but the gray light is now brighter.

"There they are," John whispers, pointing out my window, thick fingers protruding from fingerless gloves. "They're close."

Indeed they are. Within twenty-five yards or so. Standing, sitting, lying. A peaceful pack moment. We climb out, taking care to close our doors quietly and keep the boot crunching to a minimum in the snow-covered pullout. John slides binoculars from the case strapped around his chest, rests his elbows on the hood of his truck, and studies the wolves that are now walking the road.

"Oh, cool," John exclaims, "one of them just peed on that snow pole! We're going to have to check that out."

Everything is sacred for a true wolf watcher.

A few weeks ago, I was with another instructor and we snowshoed his group to a vacant wolf den. Beside a large conifer near the den, he dropped to his knees and sniffed the tree trunk. When the rest of us giggled, he explained that he was smelling the urine with which the wolves that had used this den marked their territory. He invited us to take turns sniffing. Only one woman and I took him up on his offer. The urine smell was not unpleasant and was quite different from the musky fox urine I had smelled elsewhere a couple days earlier.

From the Rick Radio, McIntyre directs Doug, "Let me know if there are any issues with traffic."

With the wolves now on the road, McIntyre is on high alert for vehicles and the danger they present. It's a tough job; the wolves won't listen to him and neither will some drivers.

This 52-mile length of road through the park is the only way that snowmobilers—driving big pickups and pulling bigger trailers—can get to their noisy, high-speed, sometimes-dangerous fun on the steep slopes and closed-for-winter roads around Cooke City, just outside the park's northeast entrance. I've white-knuckled the steering wheel when a snowmobiler's truck and trailer passed on a curve my bus full of passengers. I've shaken my head as an impatient snowmobiler barged his truck into a herd of road-walking bison, forcing them to scatter in all directions and waste precious energy. I've held my breath as snowmobilers zoomed past pullouts overflowing with wolf watchers. A clear cultural clash exists between those snowmobilers, who see the Lamar Valley as an obstacle to overcome, and wolf watchers, who see it as a quiet place of worship.

McIntyre approaches John, concern for the wolves evident in his frown. He scratches his head through a green wool cap with a National Park Service emblem on the front. That and the badge on his jacket give him the authority to tell visitors what to do. But wolves speak a different language.

"I may have to haze them off the road if traffic picks up," he says. "Let's see what develops." He heads back to his SUV.

Hazing wolves is rare: only used, for example, four times in one recent year. Initial hazing could involve McIntyre yelling, clapping his hands, or honking the SUV horn. If that fails, he could call in rangers trained in last-resort hazing. They might use "cracker shells" that make a loud bang when fired from a shotgun. Or they might shoot a wolf with rubber bullets. Most of the time, this extreme hazing succeeds in turning a problem wolf around without harming the animal.

Still leaning on his pickup hood, John focuses his binoculars on the Lamar Canyon pack. "That's 754, I think.

He's the beta male. Look at the way he's limping. And there's the black pup that got beat up a couple of days ago by the Mollie's."

John, like other instructors, takes pride in recognizing individual wolves and knowing their history and current physical condition. That is no small task. The thirty or so wolves wearing collars provide data on the whereabouts of each collared wolf and its pack. Every wolf with a collar is assigned a number—like 754, the beta male. In addition, wolves are under constant observation from the ground and regularly viewed from the air. Even dead wolves supply data when the Wolf Project analyzes their bones, teeth, and DNA. By sifting and sorting that data, the Wolf Project discovers where wolves live, when they travel, what they eat, with whom they mate, and why they fight. It's not a stretch to say that the Wolf Project knows more about these wolves than some parents know about their children.

Squinting with concentration, John stares at a soaring raven.

"What are you looking for?" I ask.

"To see if he has anything in his beak. If he does, he's flying away from a kill to cache it. If he doesn't, then maybe he's flying back to it."

Either way, that raven could help John find a wolf kill. And if he finds a kill, he may find wolves. In that sense, he is little different than our distant ancestors, the early hunters who also followed ravens to wolf kills in order to secure their share of the wolves' bounty.

As my mind caches this tracking tidbit, I see McIntyre slip back into his SUV. Then I hear him on the radio, in cryptic words trying to determine if Doug can see wolves coming up the road. Doug says he can, but only if he steps out of his car. McIntyre asks him to get back into his car. Wolves are so accustomed to vehicles—so habituated to them—that cars make good blinds from which to observe, but not bother, the animals.

The wolves' familiarity with human contraptions and McIntyre's fear of habituation remind me of a comment I heard last night in the bunkhouse. A young, seasonal park ranger, intelligent eyes framed by stylish, black-rimmed glasses, asked John, "Do you think the wolves here are *wild* animals?" John rubbed his hand over his buzz-cut hair and replied, "That's a good question. I'm not sure."

Thinking now about this road, the cars, and the wolves, I wonder for the first time if the Lamar Valley is in danger of becoming just another drive-through wildlife safari.

John rescues me from that disturbing image when he says, "I count ten wolves, so the pack's probably missing the light gray male. He's out looking for love, I've heard. That can be a very dangerous move. He may stumble into another pack and get killed."

I struggle to recall the term for wolves that leave their packs. I read it the other night, but today it escapes my aging brain. "There's a word for that," I mutter.

John drops the binoculars, smiles at me, and says, "Horny."

I laugh at a side of John, his humor, he doesn't reveal to participants. Then the word I seek pops into my head. "Disperser!" I proclaim.

"Oh, yeah, that's it." He grins and then slips into his instructor role. "When they leave their pack they're called a disperser, and when they enter a new pack they're called an interloper."

The radio interrupts our banter. Doug says he sees some, but not all, of the wolves. They're in the road, but no traffic is coming. McIntyre replies that he'll drive toward the wolves, perhaps to encourage them off the road. Then McIntyre instructs John to pull his truck into the road and stop.

McIntyre drives away at a slow speed, flashers going, yellow SUV bright in the light snow. We pull into the road and park. John's truck is now a blockade protecting the wolves from the west. Doug's SUV blocks traffic from the east. The wolves are bookended safely, but that can't last for long.

"Unit Six, you can drive my way." McIntyre again. "You'll see them off to your left. The best thing would be to go to the next pullout, but if you want to stop for a moment to take a shot, that wouldn't be the end of the world." McIntyre is rewarding John with a photo op for volunteering his time—as John has this morning and on many others—to assist the Wolf Project.

We roll forward and spot the wolves silhouetted on a hill beside the road. The pack has come together into a rally, bumping and tumbling, tails wagging, happy to be reunited. McIntyre sounds relieved when he confirms that all members of the pack are present.

We turn into Coyote pullout, which is becoming—as predicted—clogged with cars. Despite the early hour and the efforts to be secretive, visitors have deduced that the Lamar

Canyon pack is near the road. We set up a spotting scope, too. But we can't stay long; the sun is almost over Druid Peak. Those excited new participants back at the ranch must have finished their breakfast by now and are checking the time, anxious to board the bus and start wolf watching.

John and I don't yet know about the surprise in store for us—and them—at today's sunrise service.

13

Trapped by Wolves

———

Across the snow-covered valley floor from the ranch, the Lamar Canyon pack encircles a bull elk. He has backed up against a large, uprooted stump and stands with his front hooves in a shallow braid of Rose Creek. He is six-feet tall at the shoulder with 6 X 6 antlers and far from defenseless. He has several ways to kill a careless wolf.

The elk and wolves are less than a half mile from us, visible with the naked eye and amazingly detailed through the spotting scopes that I am rushing to help participants set up for this surprising sunrise service. John spotted this stand-off moments ago, just after he and I had returned from helping Rick McIntyre on the road, and before our twenty Wolf Week participants boarded the buses.

The air buzzes with excited chatter about how this life-or-death drama may unfold; wolves succeed in only one of every five attempts. The pack's last confirmed kill was three days ago, a long dry spell for them. They have been gnawing on bones at old kill sites, and must be famished. Feasting on this elk who may weigh 900 pounds is crucial—but not guaranteed.

This elk could be a good choice for two reasons. First, a big elk means more meat per wolf. Second, a bull this big is probably exhausted after last fall's rut during which he may have collected a large harem of cows. While not mating with the cows, he was busy scanning for, or fending off, other bulls. He slept little, expended lots of energy, and did not graze enough to completely recharge. After the rut ended, he went off to live by himself all winter. Thus he had little time to build up enough fat to survive the hardest season of the year. Now, after several months of below-freezing temperatures, deep snow, and poor grazing, he could be even more depleted, more vulnerable to these hungry wolves.

As I walk from scope to scope, checking in with participants, I overhear a trickle of uncertainty diluting their initial flood of excitement. A few people are starting to wonder whether they want to see the wolves bring down the elk.

I don't like the idea of this brave and beautiful elk dying either, but I have learned that when the wolf eats, everyone eats. Researchers have estimated how a wolf kill is parceled out. A pack member can "wolf down" twenty pounds. A coyote may take eight, an eagle three, and a raven two. Then there are grizzly bears, famished when they emerge from hibernation. A bear will run the wolves off, monopolize the kill, and may even lie down and sleep on it. After the bear has its fill and leaves, coyotes, ravens, magpies, and bald eagles return and feast until only hide and bones remain. Eventually hundreds of types of beetles and other insects will consume those meager leftovers.

As I adjust one man's scope, he asks, "Does standing in the creek give the elk an advantage?"

"Unfortunately, not today," I reply. "That only helps if the water is so deep that the wolves have to swim."

As I am finishing the adjustment, the wolves crouch, charge, and nip at the elk's legs. I step aside from the scope, and the man jumps into my place and zooms in as the elk, head up, charges. The wolves retreat. The elk backs into the creek.

After this give and take repeats several times, the man says with obvious admiration, "It's like he's using the creek as home base in a game of tag."

The first round of this game ends with the wolves curling up in the snow in a long, loose line that starts near the elk and stretches eastward. Though the temperature is below freezing, they look like dogs sleeping on the hearth. All except for 06, the alpha female. Although positioned at the end of the line and farthest from the elk, she never takes her eyes off him. The elk, head high, still as a statue, glares right back.

As the stand-off settles into a staring match, many of us leave the spotting scopes and sit in a line of our own on blue foam pads that we have placed on a snow bank. We make quiet small talk and wait for whatever the wolves or elk will do next.

When 06 finally stands and stretches, I am back at my own scope, blowing into my cupped hands and stamping my feet. The black alpha male, his black larger brother, and two younger wolves join her and move toward the elk. With no hesitation, the elk charges, making the wolves dodge and feint. 06 moves to the elk's front. She's famous among wolf watchers for lunging at an elk's neck, crushing its windpipe, and hanging on till the elk suffocates. Is that what she's going to do now? Or is she trying to entice him to chase her? If he chases, his unprotected rear becomes a perfect target for the rest of the pack. Those bites would not kill him outright, but if he bleeds, he'll weaken. That would make delivering the eventual death blow easier, and the wolves would eat at last. But this elk is experienced; he stands his ground and protects his back. The wolves return to resting, again curling up in the snow. Score round two for the elk.

Hans and Julie, two staff members of the Wolf Project, set up their scopes near us. This is the pack that they're assigned to study for the month of March. They watch these animals daily from sunrise to sunset. The tracking collar on 06 also allows them to follow her movements, day or night, even when they can't see her. Because of that, Hans and Julie may know more than we do about this encounter.

When I ask them what they know, Julie says, "We think the wolves forced this elk down to the valley floor last night from higher up." She motions for me to look in her scope. "If you focus in on his right rear leg, you'll see a bloody notch where they bit him."

I adjust her scope and sure enough, there's the notch with blood stains below it. I step away and say, "I can't believe that he's going to survive this."

Hans says that he just spoke to Bob Landis, the film-maker, who arrived about an hour after the stand-off started.

He has set up his large video camera on the roof of a van. The footage he captures of this encounter will likely end up on TV or in a movie. I want to hear what Landis told Hans since Landis has spent more time observing Yellowstone's wildlife than anyone else I'll ever meet. Hans says that Landis has seen this kind of situation before, and about half the time the elk walks away.

I shake my head in amazement and respect for the elk. "Ten hungry wolves led by the best hunter in the valley, and this elk's going to get away? Incredible."

While the wolves rest, I cross the short distance from the parking lot to the warm bunkhouse for a hot cup of coffee. Inside, I find others of my group, taking a break from the cold and the intensity of the stand-off. As I stand alone, enjoying how drinking coffee warms my hands and my insides, I overhear one man whisper to his friend, "I'm not sure I want to see anymore." The friend glances around the room, perhaps to see if anyone is listening, and then whispers that he agrees.

So many people from so many countries journey here to see wolves in their wild freedom. But not all want to see wolves feast in their bloody glory. If I drew a line now in the parking lot and asked those in favor of the wolves to stand on one side, those for the elk to stand on the other, the two groups might be equal in size.

Put me on the side of favoring the wolves but not because I'm bloodthirsty. I volunteer here with the goal of observing as much as possible about this ecosystem and the food web. During the winter, wolves are the top predators and everyone—from beetles to bears—benefits. Though I have spent countless hours watching wolves this winter, I have yet to witness a pack bring down prey. After the two days spent earlier this season watching coyotes eat the bison calf, I think I could watch with a naturalist's eye as the wolves brought down this elk and began the feast in which so many creatures participate.

I gulp the last of my coffee and head back outside. Walking toward my scope, I see the elk move. When I reach the scope, I can't pull my eyes away as the elk backs up a few steps and then stops. He watches the wolves. They don't move. He backs away again. Stops. Stares. Three wolves raise their heads. None stands. The elk turns and with no pursuit strides away, a hundred yards, a quarter mile, a half mile. He stops. This bull looks experienced, and the chances of seeing the wolves bring him down are diminishing.

"Are they just going to let him leave?" I ask Julie.

She shrugs. So does Hans. If they don't know what the wolves are going to do, there's only one other person to ask: Rick McIntyre, the Archbishop. Lucky for me, he has just arrived. I join him where he stands apart from the crowd, whispering observations into his digital voice recorder, increasing that word count. I wait until he has finished and then ask if he thinks the elk has escaped, if the feast has fled.

He studies the animals then turns to me. "Oh, this isn't over," he says with a smile. "The pack will have no trouble tracking that elk later."

I feel like smacking my forehead and yelling "Duh!" Of course these noses-on-four-legs can track this animal. Why didn't I think of that? I couldn't even qualify as an altar boy in this temple. Embarrassed but still curious, I ask, "Do you think the wolves know this elk?"

"Very likely they do. Either by scent or appearance. This is probably not his first encounter with the pack. He's old enough to have had others. And he's fit enough to survive this one, too."

McIntyre turns back to his scope, grabs the voice recorder, and whispers a few notes. He's back at work, and my visit is over.

As I turn to leave, somebody yells, "The wolves are up!"

I snap my head toward the stand-off and see the wolves, noses to the snow, drifting the half mile to where the bull stands, a cliff now protecting his rear. I sprint to my scope (as much as you can when wearing heavy, insulated boots) and zoom in. The wolves form a horseshoe around the elk who charges one; it scoots away, but a second leaps at his rear. The bull spins and lowers his head, shakes his thorny rack side to side. A wolf could die if an antler punctures an internal organ. The whole pack backs off and settles down to rest. The elk takes round three.

This match has been on for five hours this morning and who knows for how long last night. Though the elk seems to be standing his ground, I wonder if he is in fact losing ground. His body must be firing adrenaline and burning energy at a high rate. But we have yet to see him eat, drink, or rest. The once-again-resting wolves may be winning this battle of energy attrition.

An hour or so later, the elk lies down. Instantly, 06 is on her feet, charging and nipping. The elk jumps up. Other hungry wolves join in until there are eight of them, circling and snapping.

"This might be it!" a woman shouts.

The elk lashes out with a front hoof. A hoof to a wolf's head can mean instant death, and one to a wolf's side can lead to slow death from internal bleeding. Trying to feast can be fatal. The wolves give ground. The elk takes round four.

At 6 p.m., eleven hours since we set up our scopes, 06 stands and saunters past the elk and down the valley. It's a determined walk, one that says this hunt is over. Perhaps— as McIntyre said—she knows this bull and has decided that bringing him down right now isn't worth the energy or risk. Whatever her motive, the other wolves fall in line behind her. The elk, defiant to the last, charges a couple of youngsters who come too close as they pass.

The wolves' stomachs must be growling as they climb a slope and leave the valley floor after yet another day without food. But at the ridge top, all ten join in a rough-and-tumble reunion. They've drawn blood, and none of the pack was injured. Though they haven't feasted, they'll live to hunt another day.

The elk stands and watches them before he meanders a short distance to graze where dried grass pokes through snow. I'm surprised that he makes no attempt to leave this dangerous area. Does he figure that the danger has left him? Or is he just too drained?

With the wolves gone, McIntyre, Hans, Julie, and Landis jump into their cars and leave. The seminar participants turn from the scopes and head to the bunkhouse for its warmth and their dinner. I collect the scopes, collapse the legs of the tripods, and return the equipment to the bunkhouse. By the time I enter the dining room it is spiced with the aroma of pot roast and resounds with passionate debate: Do you want the wolves to succeed or the elk to escape? You can't have both! Opinions are hotly mixed.

But this morning—when we first spotted the stand-off—almost everyone was excited about the possibility of watching wolves hunt. Over the course of a long day, some people grew ambivalent about seeing the wolves kill the elk. Others became adamant that they would not want to witness such a violent act. But I don't recall anyone leaving when eight wolves were circling and biting and we thought the end was near.

Whether they want to or not, few visitors to Yellowstone ever see wolves feasting; fewer still are lucky enough to see wolves bring down prey. With the chance to witness both, we were as trapped by the wolves as that elk.

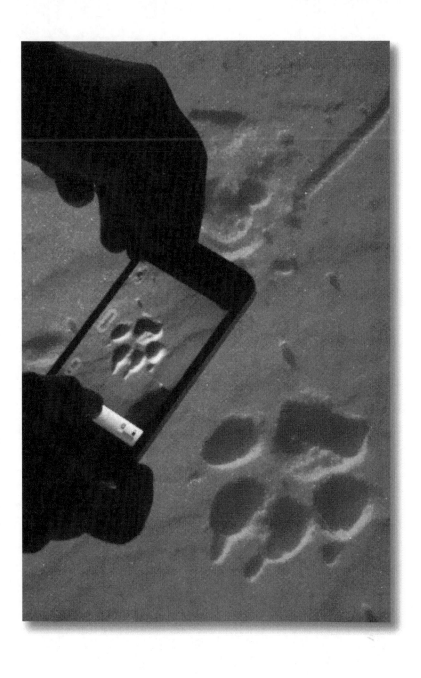

14

The Kill

———

Early the next morning, Mary and I slip and slide up the muddy, snowy, and rocky flank of Ranger Hill. Last night we heard a lot of wolf howling. At breakfast we learned that a conspiracy of ravens and an eagle were circling in the area of the stand-off. Was it a victory chorus of meat-drunk wolves? We're climbing for a view, to see if there's a carcass.

Halfway up the hill, Mary sits on the edge of a lichen-dotted rock outcrop, feet dangling, blond hair blowing in the breeze. She searches with binoculars. I set up the scope and start scanning but see no movement.

A moment later, Mary whispers with reverence, "Got it. Wolves on a kill. Lots of ravens. Right below that lone conifer across the valley."

I follow her directions and zoom in on 06 pulling a strip of meat from a carcass that's halfway submerged in Rose Creek. A raven perches on the antlers. I count twelve points. This must be the big guy from yesterday, the one who shook those antlers defiantly at the pack. McIntyre was right: 06 wasn't done when the wolves walked away.

Our curiosity satisfied, we head back to the ranch; there's work to do. At mid-afternoon, I take a break from the cabin I'm cleaning, head outside, and run into Hans and Julie. They tell me that the Lamar Canyon pack has now moved off the kill and are bedded down far to the east.

"Do you know how the kill happened?" I ask.

Julie nods with excitement. "We monitored 06 by radio telemetry after she left the elk yesterday. Once the pack was out of sight, she circled back toward the elk."

"So the pack made the kill at night?"

"Yes," Julie says. "And interestingly it took place in almost the exact same spot as where he had made his stand the day before. He was probably standing in the creek when he was taken down."

"How old do you think he was?" I ask.

Hans replies, "We're not sure yet. But once the wolves are done feeding, we'll head out and do the necropsy. That'll give us more info."

He's referring to the postmortem that the Wolf Project conducts on most known kills. The team will study, for example, the elk's teeth and estimate his age by wear. They'll saw open a big leg bone and sample the bone marrow to gauge his health.

After work, Mary and I cross the road and wind our way along Rose Creek, in search of the carcass. As I'm telling her that I'm surprised the kill happened at night, that I thought wolves hunted only at dawn and dusk, we round a corner and see the distant kill. A coyote slinks around it, looking for some meat. A bald eagle with a hoof and bone dangling from its talons flies over the stump that the elk used yesterday for defense. If we continue toward the kill site, we may interrupt the scavengers' meal. We don't want to do that so we return to the ranch.

In the evening we attend a program featuring Rick McIntyre as the guest speaker. As the Archbishop describes the Lamar Canyon pack's genealogy—who begat whom—he sounds like he is preaching from the Old Testament. When he concludes his talk, I ask how common it is for wolves to hunt at night. He says that they prefer it. Their night vision is better than an elk's so they have the advantage. Their sense of smell is so strong that they can find prey in the dark. Last night, they may have tracked the bull by the scent from his bloody wound.

The next day I am on camp duty again and run into Julie outside the bunkhouse. "How'd the necropsy go?" I ask.

She sounds like a doctor on rounds. "He was six years old. The marrow was gelatinous and normal for a bull this time of year. The teeth were fine. There weren't many bones left at the kill site."

"So he was young and healthy?"

"Yes, he was. But 06 wouldn't let him rest. He must have been very tired from the stand-off. And he had lost blood from the bites." Julie nods her head in admiration. "She's really good at that kind of kill."

A couple of days later, I have the day off and climb to the top of Ranger Hill. The group that watched the stand-off has left the temple and the next Wolf Week worshippers have not yet arrived. More snow has fallen, chasing away the first hints of spring, and the valley is once again a pure-white canvas. The wind is chilly, but I find a protected spot and settle down. I look out to where the wolves killed the elk. All the facts and opinions that I've heard about wolves and elk in the last few days tumble around in my head. I consider the sources: the participants, emotional spectators; Hans, Julie, and McIntyre, trained observers. Each saw the event through his or her own filter.

I lean back, turn my face to the setting sun, close my eyes, and whisper aloud, "What about the elk? What was it like for him?" My imagination takes over.

It's dark, the half-moon not yet up, when the bull first senses the wolves approaching. He can't see them, but he can smell their damp, dirty coats. He hears the crunch of a paw breaking through the snow's crust. He knows he needs to get ready.

He trots toward Rose Creek and enters the water. It's warmer than the air at first, but as he stands there, he can feel it sucking heat from his body. And energy. Precious energy that he's not been able to replace in the few hours of grazing he's had since the pack left. He's not as strong as he could be. He waits.

A short while later he hears the first growl. It's the gray wolf, the fierce female who wouldn't let him lie down yesterday. Behind her are the two blacks. They're not as smart as the female, but they're big and strong. The rest of the pack doesn't worry him much; they're young, inexperienced, and pose little danger.

The pack wastes no time. The gray lunges at his rear, trying to get him to run. But the elk knows better. He spins and charges; she backs away, canines bared, growling. While he's turned, one of the black males leaps and bites high on his right rear leg, close to where he was bitten last night. He feels the fire for fighting course through his body. He spins, throws the male off, and comes face to face with the larger black. He drops his head, shows him his antlers.

A pup lunges at his side, bites but can't get a grip, falls into the water, and rolls away, splashing. Another pup growls and snaps and edges closer. The big blacks close in. The bull prepares to lash out with a front hoof.

But before he can kick, he feels terrific pain; the gray female has jumped up and bitten deep into his rear. He bucks and feels her fall away, hears her grunt as she hits the bank. He spins to face her, raises his head in a show of strength, and bugles.

The gray leaps, and he feels her strong jaws lock on his neck, her canines break through hide and crunch his windpipe shut. He ducks and spins and bucks but can't shake her, can't get air either. The big wolf swinging from his neck throws him off balance; he pitches forward, front knees splashing into the water. The two blacks jump onto his back. Their weight buckles his rear legs. The pack swarms, covering him in a frenzy of biting and ripping. He's burning with pain until the lack of air shuts his brain down. His limp body tumbles sideways into the creek.

I open my eyes and shudder. The sun has set and the wind has picked up. Time to make my way down. I stand and stretch and admire this wild place, this temple where I have come to worship and learn. Picking my way down the hill in the fading light, I hear a wolf howl. Is that 06, rounding up the pack for another night of hunting? I imagine another elk hearing the howl and raising his majestic rack toward the sky, alert, watching, waiting. Will he be the next blood sacrifice in this temple of wolves?

15

The Cash Cascade

On some evenings after dinner, as we relax around the table in the bunkhouse and recall the day's sightings, the talk drifts to wolves and the impact of their return to Yellowstone. I listen closely as scientists, instructors, park rangers, and wolf watchers describe how wolves have changed the lives of animals such as coyotes, elk, and beaver for better or worse.

But sometimes as others talk, I mentally drift away, lost in thoughts of how wolves have impacted that other Yellowstone animal, the human. I find myself concentrating on one particular impact: financial. I can't help myself; I have an MBA.

I wasn't always a $12-a-day-volunteer. Before I retired, I used my degree and consulted to individuals and companies. I analyzed numbers and found that while figures don't tell the whole story, statistics can reveal either profitable or dangerous trends.

When I think like an MBA about the return of wolves, I stop considering only their ecological impact and also ask myself: How has the return of wolves helped locals make or lose money?

Earlier in this book, I described one theory—Trophic Cascade—that explains the wolves' ecological impact. According to that theory, whether wolf reintroduction was good or bad depends on the animal considered. Elk would not be cheering; wolves have made their lives harder. Beavers, on the other hand, are slapping their tails with joy.

I have developed my own theory about the wolves' financial impact, and, with a nod to Trophic Cascade, I call it the Cash Cascade. Whether that cascade is good or bad depends on who counts the cash.

The businesses in small towns surrounding the park are happily counting increased profits from the additional visitors who come in search of wolf sightings. According to a Montana State University study, close to half of the Yellowstone visitors surveyed said that the wolf was the animal that they would most like to see. That's second only to the number of visitors who want to see grizzlies.

The study also calculated how much money these wolf-hungry visitors pumped into the local economy. Depending on the season, an average visitor coming from outside the area seeking a view of Yellowstone's wolves left $361 to $510 behind in Idaho, Montana, and Wyoming. Over the course of a year, visitors coming with this intent pumped $35 million into that three-state area.

The Wolf Weeks are a prime example of how this cash cascades. Those three seminars will draw a total of sixty people, more than any other topic all winter. Every wolf watcher plunks down about $600 for the seminar and $120 for lodging. That's more than $43,000 cascading into the coffers of the Yellowstone Association. YA, in turn, pays local caterers to feed the visitors, guides to lead them, and the ranch manager to control the crowd.

But that's only part of the cascade. Wolf Week visitors open their wallets at the small YA store at the ranch and the big one in Gardiner. They buy books, DVDs, clothing, coffee cups, stickers, and more. YA profits from each sale as do the authors, filmmakers, publishers, manufacturers—you name it—right on down the retailing chain.

And more cash cascades as the visitors travel to and from the park. Many fly into Bozeman, rent a car, and drive to Yellowstone, filling up with fuel and food along the way. At the gate outside Gardiner, they pay the National Park Service entry fee.

YA is not the only tour operator in the park. There are others, and one told *Outside Magazine* that it grossed $500,000 in a recent year.

The return of wolves has, in fact, given local businesses another profitable season: winter. A small home-based photography gallery near the park's northeastern entrance is a good example. The owner told me that when the gallery opened more than twenty years ago, summer sales were good, but winter sales were almost non-existent. Then the wolves returned. Since 1995, winter sales have increased so much that they now exceed those of summer.

Tourism is just one braid of the cash cascade into the three-state area. *Yellowstone Science* reports that the scientific monitoring of wolves brings in $1.5 million a year. The reintroduction in 1995 and 1996 pumped in $870,000. Most of that money must have gone to the salaries of people living in or around the park.

On the other hand, ranchers in Idaho, Montana, and Wyoming claim that cash has cascaded out of—not into—their bank accounts since the wolves returned. And they have a point: Wolves have killed their livestock. Between 1987 and 2009, 1120 cattle, 2338 sheep, and 82 other animals were confirmed as wolf kills in the three-state area.

As an MBA, I can't help but wonder: Do those numbers represent a large or small cost of doing business as a rancher?

According to a 2005 study published in *Yellowstone Science*, the number of livestock lost to wolves was less than one percent of the total of all livestock in the parts of Idaho, Montana, and Wyoming near Yellowstone. That's a minor financial cost of doing business.

But some ranchers claim that those monetary losses—even if small—have a much greater emotional impact. Here's how one, Cody Lockhart, put it in an interview with the BBC. While standing in the pasture of his family ranch south of Yellowstone, he said that wolves were not a huge problem until the last few years when they began killing his cattle and attacking his dogs. He said that it's hard to stomach waking up in the morning to find the wolf-killed carcass of an animal his family has raised. He added, "We certainly should have the right to protect our way of life, our animals. And if that means killing or shooting a few wolves when they are in our backyard or on our land, I certainly think that's something that we need to have the right to do."

I believe that Lockhart is sincere in his description of the emotional impact on his family from wolves killing their animals. I also believe that he is sincere in his desire to kill wolves to protect his livestock. But his words "protect our way of life" keep running through my mind. I can't help but wonder if wolves are all that's endangering the ranching way of life or whether there are other trends at work.

By viewing ranching as a business, I have learned that there are many ways ranchers can lose cattle and profits, and thus also lose their way of life. The U.S. Department of Agriculture tracks cattle and calf deaths due to a variety of predator and non-predator causes. They issue a report every five years and the most recent one covers losses in 2010. After spending hours analyzing those statistics, I've come to believe that cattle ranching is a much riskier occupation than I first thought. From calving problems to respiratory illness to weather, the morbid list of cattle killers goes on and on. Wolves are but one of many, many risks.

But the question remains: Are wolves a significant-enough risk to threaten the ranching way of life?

Nationally, losses of cattle due to non-predator causes such as disease, poisoning, and theft far outweigh losses attributed to wolves. In terms of predators, the losses caused by dogs are greater than losses from wolves. As are the losses from vultures, mountain lions, or coyotes. Nationally then, wolves are one of a rancher's smaller risks.

The picture in Idaho, Montana, and Wyoming is similar to and yet different from the national situation. As happens nationally, ranchers in the three-state area lose far more cattle to non-predator causes than they lose to predators. The USDA reports that in Montana in 2010, for example, ranchers lost 22,000 head of cattle to non-predator causes and only 1,000 head to predators.

But the picture differs in the three-state area in an important way: In Idaho, Montana, and Wyoming wolves are responsible for the majority of predator losses. Wolves kill more cattle than do dogs, vultures, mountain lions, or coyotes.

So local ranchers have a right to complain about wolves, and they have an obligation to protect their herds. But protection doesn't necessarily require killing wolves. There are many nonlethal tactics that ranchers can use. They can increase human presence with guard dogs or range riders or herders. They can pen livestock at night in small pens rather than leaving them vulnerable in large, difficult-to-defend pastures. Ranchers can cull weak, injured, or sick animals from the herd since those are wolf favorites. They can remove the carcasses of animals that die of natural causes instead of leaving them to rot in the field and attract wolves. Ranchers can train their cattle to bunch up in smaller, tighter herds, which are less attractive to wolves. They can install fencing that is better at keeping out wolves. And ranchers can use fright tactics such as installing alarms triggered by the radio collars that some wolves wear, or putting shock collars on wolves that hunt near ranches, or firing non-lethal ammunition like the cracker shells used to haze wolves in Yellowstone.

The USDA gives a national average for the use of each tactic. Idaho, Montana, and Wyoming ranchers employ herding, night penning, fright tactics, and carcass removal more than the national average. Idaho and Montana use culling more than the national average. Idaho and Wyoming use frequent checks of the herd more. Ranchers in these three states are working hard at using nonlethal means to keep wolves away from their cattle. And, no doubt, those extra efforts cost money and reduce profits.

But by how much?

Here is where a private organization, Defenders of Wildlife, enters the picture. Between 1987 and 2009, Defenders operated a Wolf Compensation Trust with this stated goal: "...to shift the economic response for wolf recovery away from individual ranchers and toward the millions of people who want to see the wolf population restored. When ranchers alone are forced to bear the cost of wolf recovery, it creates animosity and ill will toward the wolf. Such negative attitudes can result in illegal killing."

Those negative attitudes appear in Idaho, Montana, and Wyoming in sayings and bumper stickers such as, "Smoke a Pack a Day," "Track and Whack," "Help Preserve a Wolf, Take One to a Taxidermist," or "Shoot, Shovel, and Shut Up" (abbreviated as SSS in caustic letters to the editors of local papers).

To reduce the animosity, the Wolf Compensation Trust during those twelve years paid ranchers in the three-state area $1.2 million for wolf-related livestock losses. That was 89% of the total trust payout; the rest went to ranchers in

Arizona, New Mexico, and Oregon. Regardless of where they lived, that compensation must have boosted the bottom line of ranchers. In 2010 Defenders of Wildlife stopped paying ranchers because public money became available to help individual states operate similar compensation programs.

When viewed as part of the bigger picture, the losses of livestock to wolves are only one of many risks ranchers face. And ranchers can be compensated for most wolf-related losses.

So, if wolves are not killing the ranching way of life, what is?

One possible culprit is that Americans are eating less beef. Between 2002 and 2011 the amount of beef consumed in the U.S. fell eight percent. As demand dropped, the number of cattle on ranches across the U.S. dropped six percent.

But ranchers in Idaho, Montana, and Wyoming fared better. While the number of cattle on ranches elsewhere fell, the amount of cattle on ranches in the three-state area increased. And it did so in spite of the wolf population in those same three states tripling from 663 in 2002 to 1727 in 2011. Local ranchers—with wolves near or in their pastures—are doing better than ranchers elsewhere.

As I ponder the Cash Cascade, there's no doubt that ranchers have seen cash flow out of their operations as they spend more to protect their herds. But the losses, in my view, do not support the volume of the ranchers' rallying cry to protect their profits and way of life by killing wolves.

I cannot help but think that there is something else involved here. Something not measured by statistics,

something that lives almost DNA-deep within many of us—
not just ranchers. That something else is a hatred of wolves
that goes well beyond the actual impact these animals have
on us. Though that hatred cannot be measured, it amplifies
the intensity of ranchers' complaints and clouds the view of
the actual financial impact of wolf reintroduction.

16

Creating a World of Wolf Haters

———

From the United States to the United Kingdom, from Europe to Japan, wolves have been hated to death. I struggle to believe that humans haven't always hated wolves. Yet some experts say that long ago—when we were nomadic and had limitless horizons—wolves and humans coexisted peacefully and even evolved together. How did we get from that to a world of wolf haters?

One theory, from Mark Derr, author of *How the Dog Became the Dog*, proposes that fifteen to twenty thousand years ago nomadic hunters following game could have encountered a pack of wolves. The hunters and wolves did not fight or flee. Instead, some of those humans and wolves were right for one another, were both sociable and curious. Those wolves were capable of overcoming fear of a creature from another species and making what Derr calls "a leap of friendship."

After that leap, our ancient ancestors learned from the wolves. They observed packs hunting herds of prey and adopted some of the wolves' tactics. The new approaches produced more meat than the hunters could consume or carry and they left the excess. Wolves ate their fill and tasted how they could benefit from humans. Those hunters had begun the long process of domesticating man's worst enemy, *Canis lupus*, into man's best friend, *Canis lupus familiaris*.

Derr's image of two intelligent and resourceful creatures meeting on a trail, befriending one another, and evolving together places the wolf in a much-needed positive light. Wolves that eventually became dogs were not, as the prevailing theory goes, rejects from their packs that slinked around in the shadows of the nomads' campfires and begged for food. This distinction is important. Which would you respect and value more: an animal capable of making a leap of friendship or a reject begging for a handout?

Derr's wolves chose to enter into a partnership with humans, and both parties benefitted. But that partnership started to unravel eight to ten thousand years ago as hunters became herders. No longer a nomad with a limitless horizon, a herder's territory shrank to the confines of a small patch of land. His family survived on what that patch produced. Any animal that ate the herder's sheep, goats, pigs, or cattle took food from the family and reduced their chances of survival.

Those parcels of land were often in wolf territory where wolves did what they still do best: pick the easiest prey possible. So when herders put their livestock in those pastures, they were feeding them to the wolves. That killing of livestock changed our relationship with *Canis lupus* forever. We were no longer two species coexisting. We were two species competing.

Stepping back and viewing ourselves as *Homo sapiens*, members of a competitive species, allows us a different perspective on wolf hate. From that view, we do not detest the wolf because it is an evil animal. Our hatred is a symptom of interspecies conflict with wolves for territory and food. In that sense, I see our relationship with the wolf as similar to the wolf's relationship with the coyote.

Wolves I've watched in Yellowstone are a perfect example of this. When a pack brings down an elk, each member eats its fill and then moves away from the carcass to sleep off the "meat drunk." As the wolves drowse, an opportunistic coyote may sneak in to scavenge. The wolves may pay no mind, chase the coyote, or kill the scavenger. If they kill the coyote, they usually don't eat it. The wolves are not hungry; they are just cutting the competition for their hard-won meal. Wolves and coyotes have coexisted like this for thousands and thousands of years, with careless coyotes losing their lives but their species surviving.

In the case of wolves and humans, we are the top predator. When opportunistic wolves encroach on our livestock—often while we sleep—we may do nothing, chase the wolves away, or kill, but not eat, the wolves.

Human-wolf conflict has proven inevitable for a number of reasons. Wolves live almost everywhere we do. Both species are territorial. *Canis lupus* marks territory by scent marking and howling, while *Homo sapiens* use political borders and barbed wire. Wolves and humans like the same meals, and for the same reason: A domestic cow grazing in a wide-open pasture, for example, is much easier to catch, kill, and devour than a big bull elk defending itself in a belly-deep river. Wolves can bring down that elk because they hunt in packs; they find strength in numbers. As do humans by cooperating in families and groups. Within a wolf pack or human group there are dominant and submissive members, leaders and followers.

This combination of territoriality, cooperative behavior, and dominant members leads to wars: wolves fighting wolves, humans fighting humans, and, of course, humans waging war against wolves. And make no mistake, we have waged a one-sided war; wolves rarely attack humans.

When wolves battle coyotes for food and territory, their weapons are native intelligence, speed, strength, and teeth. With those weapons, wolves leave their competitor species intact. But we have a much more varied and deadly arsenal—including biological and chemical weapons. We also have bigger—and more devious—brains as well as opposable thumbs with which we devise a frightening array of battle plans against wolves. The end result: We can exterminate all the wolves we can find.

As an arbitrary starting point in this one-sided and centuries-old war, let's begin with the Middle Ages, the 5th to the 15th century. This was a time when many horrifying rumors—some true—about rabid wolves killing humans spread across Europe. Governments, composed of the dominant members of our species, reacted. France, in the 9th century, paid an elite corps of hunters to control the wolf population. In England in the late 1200s, King Edward 1 ordered the extermination of wolves in those parts of the country where wolves were more numerous—and easier to find. In Scotland in1427, James l passed a law requiring three wolf hunts a year, some during denning season when wolves were least mobile.

Those wolf wars were not waged in a vacuum. Our ancestors were reacting as a species to environmental threats. First, near the end of the 13th century in Europe, a "Little Ice Age" chilled the continent, reducing crop harvests and creating shortages of wheat, oats, hay, and livestock. Then the Great Famine struck northwest Europe, killing about ten percent of the population. With families and friends starving and dying, no one would put up with wolves killing livestock. I can imagine the message spreading across the countryside: Wolves are our enemies. To protect ourselves and our territory we must use our arrows, spears, clubs, and pits and kill them. All of them.

Then conditions worsened: The Black Death arrived. The plague peaked in the mid-1300s and killed thirty to sixty percent of Europe's population. Once the Black Death subsided, the human population rebounded and doubled by the early 1600s. This swelling population shifted the balance of power between wolves and humans, according to Jon T. Coleman, author of *Vicious: Wolves and Men in America*. More people meant more mouths to feed. Producing more food required more land for livestock and crops. That led to stealing more wolf territory. And killing wolves.

By the early 1500s wolves had been hunted and trapped to extinction in England. They were eradicated from Scotland by the late 1600s and from Ireland by the late 1700s.

Even though Europe covers a large area, space for human expansion was limited by political boundaries. But there was a whole new world waiting across the Atlantic. By the 1600s, the colonization of North America was in full swing. When colonists disembarked in the New World, wolves were probably watching from the woods; the animals roamed most of what would become the continental United States. The stage was set for another one-sided territorial clash between two top predators.

That New World clash between *Canis lupus* and *Homo sapiens* erupted, once again, over livestock, according to Barry Lopez, in *Of Wolves and Men*. By 1625, pigs, cattle, and horses were common and colonists were working together to stop predation, using tactics learned in their home countries. In addition to digging wolf pits and building fences, colonists used firearms with which they could kill from a distance with less effort and risk. They paid professional wolf hunters and passed bounty laws—the first in Massachusetts in 1630, just ten years after the founding of the colony. Other colonies followed suit: Virginia in 1632, South Carolina in 1695, and New Jersey in 1697.

Lopez writes that by the early 1700s the colonists were moving toward self-sufficiency from England, but they needed a local wool industry to be independent. That meant raising sheep and appropriating land from wolves for pastures. As colonists encroached, wolf-human conflict increased.

In the end, wolves never fought back and could not compete with humans. Their natural intelligence, speed, strength, and teeth were no match for our big brains and big arsenals. By the early 1800s that arsenal included more powerful and accurate rifles and strychnine. This poison enabled Americans to escalate the killing of wolves to an industrial—and even more impersonal—scale. Instead of killing wolves one at a time, hunters learned that a poisoned carcass could kill an entire pack. By 1840 wolves were extinct in Massachusetts and disappearing from other states. Our one-sided war sentenced the wolf to a fate worse than we humans had suffered at the hands of the Black Death. All in a battle for territory and food.

But eliminating the animal was not enough. Even as the wolf was vanishing from the countryside, we did something that only *Homo sapiens* can do: We kept the wolf feared, hated, and alive in literature, especially children's stories.

One of the most famous collections, *Grimm's Fairy Tales*, was published in 1812 in a wolf-free Germany. Yet it contains "Little Red Riding Hood," with its infamous, conniving wolf.

Around the same time, Europeans resurrected *Aesop's Fables*, originally told more than two thousand years earlier. These stories contain tales such as "The Boy Who Cried Wolf," with its wolf that destroys the flock of a lying little boy; "The Wolf and Lamb," in which a tyrannical wolf devours an innocent lamb; and "The Wolf and Dog," in which the wolf refuses to give up its freedom to become a collared, well-fed pet, living among humans.

In 1886, more than three hundred years after the wolf was exterminated from England, "The Three Little Pigs" was published in *The Nursery Rhymes of England*. In that tale, a wolf with an insatiable appetite manages to eat two of the pigs before the third kills and eats him.

Stories such as these created a new generation of wolf haters where wolves no longer existed. Words and pictures proved to be powerful propaganda, as valuable as guns and poison in our war against wolves.

The human drive to take territory from wolves, to annihilate these competitors, and to create wolf haters is crystalized in the story of the organized eradication of the animal from Japan.

The story begins around 1600. Then, the Japanese regarded wolves as deities, worshipped them at shrines, even left ceremonial dishes of red beans and rice next to wolf dens, according to Brett Walker in his book, *The Lost Wolves of Japan.* The country had no large scale livestock industry and farmers saw the wolf as an ecological partner: The wolves killed the boars and deer that ate grain crops.

During the 1700s, the reverence for wolves diminished as the human population swelled, encroached on wolf territory, and that in turn fostered human-wolf conflict. Some rabid wolves killed humans; and all of a sudden there was a bounty on wolves and the stirring of wolf hatred.

In 1868 the Japanese government decided to stoke that stirring into a squall when it began to modernize the country's economy. At that time, modernization meant developing scientific agriculture and raising livestock on huge, new ranches, as Americans had done so successfully. Those ranches would be carved out of wolf territory. Wolves had to go.

In 1873 the Japanese government hired Edwin Dun, a rancher from Ohio, to help create the livestock industry and eradicate wolves. Dun went to work on the northern tip of Japan, on the undeveloped Hokkaido, an island just a bit smaller than Ireland. When Dun stepped off the boat with starter herds, about fifty head of cattle and a hundred sheep, the development of the livestock industry and the government's campaign to re-categorize wolves as evil predators began.

Once wolves were viewed as "noxious animals" instead of sacred deities, the next step came easy. Dun was, after all, a veteran American rancher. He knew how to eliminate wolves: bounties and strychnine.

The Japanese kept records of the rampage. By 1881, 406 wolves had been killed. By 1905, wolves were extinct. It took only thirty-two years—less than the average lifespan of a citizen—for the Japanese to go from worshipping wolves at shrines to wiping them out with strychnine. The key was when the Japanese government shifted the cultural perception of the wolf from deity to demon.

I find a question buried in this tragic tale that could lead to saving wolves. If a government can create a culture of wolf hatred and kill all wolves, can a government create a culture of wolf respect and protect wolves?

As I write this, *Canis lupus* is still on our federal endangered species list in all but a few western states. But there is a movement to remove national protection and leave wolf management to individual states. That could prove fatal for wolves. Some states with federally approved wolf management plans—and thriving livestock industries—have a culture of wolf hatred and vow to kill all wolves except the small number that their wolf management plans require they keep alive.

Plans like those barely keep wolf hatred in check and do nothing to reduce it. Plans like those give the false impression that wolf survival is a biological issue, a matter of the number of surviving breeding pairs. But wolf survival, like wolf eradication, is a cultural issue.

All federal and state wolf management plans must do more than limit the killing of wolves. They must include steps to change the long-held fundamental emotion in our culture of wolf hatred to wolf respect. We must stop seeing the animal as the Big Bad Wolf and learn to view it as a top predator that plays an essential role in nature. We must learn that the wolf is an animal we can live with, not vermin we must exterminate. Only then will the animal not be endangered.

The wolf needs real protection until we are ready to meet *Canis lupus* on the trail once again and not resort to the instinct to fight or flee. We did that once before, and our species can do it again.

17

Winter Is Leaving

All morning a determined wind has pummeled the Buffalo Ranch and the south wall of our log cabin. The wind hisses through cracks around old wooden windows, breathes down my neck, chills me as I perch on the bed just below the window sill, my back against the rough log wall.

For the last five days, I have been busy supporting the second Wolf Week. The class ended yesterday and in two days the final Wolf Week—the last seminar of the season—begins. I feel lethargic and a bit sad; the end of our stay is near.

My lazy gaze wanders across the cabin, past the rickety card table and worn folding chair where I've spent so many hours writing, past the erratic propane wall heater with its clicking, pinging, and popping, and finally through the window of the door to the tall, dry, golden grasses blown almost flat by gusts of wind. The sun's glare forces me to squint, but I can't pull my eyes away.

Just beyond our cabin's narrow porch, three-foot high piles of snow, a reminder of our months of shoveling, soften in the sun, forming long narrow puddles along the gravel walkway that is slowly re-emerging. Wind roughens the surface of the pools, whitecaps on tiny lakes.

My gaze drifts to the empty cabin across from ours. I am enthralled as the snow on the roof melts, slides down dark shingles, and drips from the roof's gutter-less edge. The wind slings the drops sideways toward Druid Peak, that ancient monolith with its enticing, inviting ridge. Along the ridge, conifers sway to the wind's rhythm. At the peak, clouds collect: gray, white, black, threatening and promising, melancholy and exquisite.

With the long, slow angling of the earth, spring is surely on its way. A few more weeks and this winter snow will be a lovely memory, a hope for next year.

18

We Are Leaving

———

The smile on my sun-warmed face widens with each ascending trill from the songbird hidden in nearby sage. I chuckle when I hear a distant reply, identical, note for note. Then, from across the narrow valley floor floats the rough purr of a Sandhill Crane. Though the thermometer says otherwise—last night's low was two below zero—these birds confirm that winter is on its way out.

And so are we. Today is March 25, the end of the winter season at the ranch. Our cabin is empty and our van is loaded. We have said goodbye to Bonnie, Karen, George, and Brian.

Hand in hand, Mary and I walk back to where I had parked the van so we could listen for birds. We climb into the van and I resume our drive toward the canyon that marks the west end of the Lamar Valley. The road is black and dry; the van's tires hum instead of the usual crunch of snow. We pass Coyote pullout crammed with excited wolf watchers staring into scopes pointed at the distant Lamar Canyon pack. We catch our last glimpse of the Archbishop, Rick McIntyre, giving an impromptu sermon to a lucky group of visitors.

One curve in the road later, bison block our way as they cross, their coats glowing in the low early-morning sun. I turn on the emergency flashers and coast to a stop. As the herd meanders in front of us, Mary and I talk about how these animals are so close to winning the race between starvation and spring. When a cow turns to look at us head-on, her big brown eyes meeting mine, her head looks too big, out of proportion with her thin body that has consumed most of its fat over the long winter.

Once the herd crosses the road, we roll on, watching the Lamar River, flowing fast and free of ice. The river descends as it enters the V-shaped canyon, not high enough for a waterfall, but enough to power a liquid saw blade that has cut through 2.6 billion-year-old rock. The river crashes and splashes around boulders still topped with snowy pillows.

Our van enters the canyon, just wide enough for the two-lane road, an occasional pullout, and the river. Once we exit this canyon, we will have left the Lamar Valley, our home for the last three months. The sadness of leaving is tinged with the excitement of reuniting with friends and family. But I still want to be fully here until the last moment, and I struggle to remain present.

I steer the van into an empty canyon pullout and we step out. We want to say goodbye to the valley. We've barely driven five miles and this is the third time we have stopped. This could be a very long ride out of the park. That should not be a surprise; they usually are, for everyone who enters this cathedral. And they always should be.

Mary strolls toward a sunny spot near the rear of the van, leans against a tree, and faces the sun. The river draws me and I pick my way along a footpath almost free of snow that switchbacks down the steep, boulder-strewn slope. My heart beats faster as I near the torrent.

I find a warm, dry boulder large enough to lie back on. I inhale and exhale slowly and my body stretches and relaxes into the dips and curves of the rock. I lock my hands behind my head and gaze at the cloudless sky. I listen to the river, feel the warmth of the sun and the chill of a breeze, smell the moist soil all around me. I want to savor every sensation this canyon offers.

I turn my eyes toward the sun's bright rays. Then I move my head ever so slightly until the trunk of a tall pine hides the sun and fashions a halo around the top of the tree. A tiny movement of my head to the left and the sun becomes a small star nestled where a thick limb joins the trunk.

The light in the valley has been one of this winter's best gifts. On some mornings, sunrise fills the sky with a blaze of yellow, orange, mauve, and red. Even on the dullest, grayest afternoons, there are thrilling moments when the sun breaks through a cloud and spotlights my favorite cottonwoods standing tall along the frozen, snow-covered Lamar River. And before the sun disappears behind Specimen Ridge, it can light the valley in a holy white glow charmed with long shadows. Sometimes I'm so overjoyed by the light that I find myself close to tears or singing love songs to the valley.

The thrills are not just visual. There's the call and response howls of wolves up and down the valley. The songs of coyotes on Ranger Hill. The grunts of bison as a herd grazes through the ranch. The calls of ravens soaring overhead. The squeak and crunch of snow underfoot. The whispers and shouts of the wind through the two ancient cottonwoods that guard the bunkhouse.

And there's the feel of the cold. The needle prick of snow blown into my face as I struggle into a thirty mile per hour wind. The way my nose hairs freeze and throat burns at ten degrees below zero. The chill as air creeps under my hood and down my back. The tingle of fingers and toes that reveals the fine line we walk in such a harsh—and beautiful—place.

Mary and I have often reminded each other how lucky we are to live and work in this wintry temple. Yellowstone has become a second home to us, and this remote corner of the park has captured our hearts in a way no other place has.

When we arrived at the ranch on New Year's Eve, I had one goal: to know this valley on a deeper level than just as magnificent scenery filled with big animals. I yearned to understand how the plants and animals fit together.

I have learned how the death of a bison calf feeds not just coyotes and ravens and magpies, but also enriches the soil hidden beneath the carcass and the snow. How that soil feeds plants that will emerge with spring's greening. How those plants will feed bees and butterflies—and bison that will produce other calves.

I've learned that everything matters here. And I want to learn more. But for that I'll have to wait nine months, until we return in the afternoon of New Year's Eve, with the sun behind us and three months of living in the snow-covered valley ahead.

Postscript

———

On a cold December day, O6, the alpha female of the Lamar Canyon pack led her family out of the park and toward the rising sun. No one knows why she chose to travel fifteen miles east of the park and into Wyoming's Wolf Trophy Game Management Area. Maybe she went in search of migrating elk. Maybe she went in search of 754, her alpha male's brother, a wolf with which she had also mated. Several weeks earlier, in the same area to which she was heading, he had become a fatality in Wyoming's first legal wolf hunt. Whatever drew her there, she never returned. On December 6, 2012, 06 became a trophy.

Wolves 06 and 754 were not the only Yellowstone wolves killed in the 2012-13 wolf hunt. A total of twelve park wolves were killed. The majority of them wore collars that provided valuable scientific information. Data from 06's collar shows that she spent ninety-five percent of her time within the park.

When Mary and I arrived for our first season at the ranch on New Year's Eve of 2011, the National Park Service counted ninety-eight wolves living in Yellowstone. One year later, the number was down to eighty. By March of 2013, the NPS count was seventy-one.

The downward trend in Yellowstone's wolf population scares me. Others, including some scientists, say there is nothing to worry about.

But no one knows how the story will unfold in this temple of wolves.

Acknowledgements

———

I'm amazed at how many people it took to write this book.

When I decided to change genres from nonfiction to creative nonfiction, I sought teachers. I found three good ones: Anne Warren Smith, C. Lill Ahrens, and Gary Ferguson. The results of their advice show up throughout *In the Temple of Wolves.*

Bonnie Quinn, campus manager, started me down the trail to the temple when she said "Yes" to Mary and me volunteering at the Lamar Buffalo Ranch. Her love and enthusiasm for the Lamar Valley are contagious. Thanks to Brian Chan for allowing us to help him take that bison calf on its last ride. George Malone, Karen Withrow, and Don MacDougall were our fellow volunteers during our first two seasons. They—along with Brian Robinson, Angela Trnka, and Mary Holleran Orr—were always willing to explore Yellowstone's wild.

While I was in the Lamar Valley, many instructors and Yellowstone Association guides—including Dan Hartman, Jim Garry, George Bumann, John Harmer, Brad Bulin, and Shauna Baron—were willing to answer my endless questions. MacNeil Lyons, Nathan Varley, and Linda Thurston of The Wild Side were also enthusiastic sources. The Yellowstone

Wolf Project staff—especially Hans and Julie—were eager to explain what I was seeing. Laurie Lyman, Doug McLaughlin, and other wolf watchers shared their knowledge and spotting scopes.

When I returned to Oregon, I began working on the journal entries I had written while at the ranch. Before submitting them as essays to literary journals and contests, they needed to be critiqued. Many thanks to Lill Ahrens and the other writers—including Dee Roy, Gary Gibson, Harry Demarest, and Ken Holt—who attended Lill's unique conversational critique classes term after term. Their critiques improved the stories. The members of the writers group to which I have belonged for several years—Dick Weinman, Brigitte Goetze, and Valerie Lake—were also instrumental in polishing the stories and helping me understand what the book was really about and why I was writing it. Dan Shapiro and I shared many evenings as he used his journalistic eye to edit my stories. Rick McIntyre read an early version of the chapters in which he appears. He caught some embarrassing mistakes and encouraged me to keep writing.

Once the stories had undergone all the changes from those reviews, I sent them to Kathleen Marusak, my editor in Los Angeles. Her editing made sure the stories read well, and her positive comments kept me going. I recommend her to any indie author.

As the book finally neared completion, I sent pre-publication copies to a few folks that know and love the Lamar Valley. Their comments cheered me on and saved me from publishing even more mistakes. I thank Terry Donnelly,

Anita Edington, Karen Withrow, Tracy Arthur, Len Carolan, Sue Timm, and Chuck Snover. Leo Leckie not only reviewed an early version of the book, he made sure my facts were straight throughout the entire writing process. I also sent a pre-publication copy to two Yellowstone experts. Bill Ripple gave me a lot of his time and helped me understand the impact of wolves on Yellowstone. Jim Halfpenny was always willing to answer questions and generous in his feedback, corrections, and comments.

While these fine folks caught mistakes (I was shocked at how many), the ones that remain (there must be a few) are mine alone.

My good friend, and exceptional photographer, Edvard Thorsett spent some of his vacation in Oregon considering the photos I had selected for possible use in the book. His comments, as well as those of my daughter, Allison, helped me choose the best ones.

Lois, my sister-in-law, spent hours listening to me read chapters and always gave heartfelt feedback—even as she struggled with a serious illness. Comments from my brother, Rus, and sister, Judy, encouraged me to develop my early "Christmas book" into this final version. My dear friends Wolfgang, Maryanne, John, and Jeanne encouraged and supported me throughout this project (and many others).

Finally, there's my wife and adventure partner, Mary. How do I begin to thank her for all that she contributed in the two years it took to finish this book? Not only did she listen to those rough—and I mean rough—journal entries, but also every subsequent version of every chapter. Her comments improved them all. And she used her sharp eye in choosing the photos as well. She supported and challenged me every step of the way. This book is dedicated to her.

About the Author

———

Essays from Rick Lamplugh's creative nonfiction about living and volunteering in Yellowstone National Park during the winter have won the 2012 Jim Stone Non-Fiction award and appeared in the literary journals *Composite Arts Magazine, Shoal,* and *Gold Man Review.* Other essays, focusing on the struggle to deal with aging, physical decline, and mortality, have appeared in the literary journals *Phoebe, Soundings Review,* and *Feathered Flounder.*

Rick lives in Oregon with his wife Mary. He hopes to observe packs of wolves in the Oregon Cascades one day.

Rick welcomes friends on Facebook and followers on Twitter. You can also check out his blog.

Blog: http://www.ricklamplugh.blogspot.com/
Facebook: https://www.facebook.com/rick.lamplugh
Twitter: https://twitter.com/rick_lamplugh

A Message to the Reader

Dear Reader,

I chose to self-publish this book because I wanted more control over the finished work. But self-publishing means that I don't have the muscle of a traditional publisher to promote the book. There's just me. And you, the satisfied reader.

You can help me—and other indie authors—by taking a moment to click onto Amazon.com and rate this book. Your star rating and review (no matter how brief) helps other readers find books by indie authors.

Thanks for reading and helping,

Rick